God is Alive and Well

Dr. Robert W. Walker

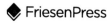
FriesenPress

Suite 300 - 990 Fort St
Victoria, BC, V8V 3K2
Canada

www.friesenpress.com

This book is written to introduce God's Spirit to each reader, who will have life
experiences that are unique to that person. Everyone has his/her relationship
with the Creator God and will follow an individual path throughout a lifetime.
The information in this book is a guide to finding the connection to God that
will bring Him/Her alive in a person's life. God is Alive and Well introduces
the concept that God and modern science come together in Einstein's quantum
mechanics but at this time cannot be totally proven scientifically.

ISBN
978-1-5255-1207-0 (Hardcover)
978-1-5255-1208-7 (Paperback)
978-1-5255-1209-4 (eBook)

1. RELIGION, SPIRITUALITY

Distributed to the trade by The Ingram Book Company

Table of Contents

Preface

God is Alive and Well introduces the reader to a totally new understanding of who God is and who we are in relation to Him/Her. The Bible states we are made in God's image but until now we have never fully understood what that means. Albert Einstein introduced us to the concept that everything in the universe is composed at the subatomic level as energy. Scientific study of quantum mechanics has proven that all energy is made up of particles of light. The Bible tells us that God is Light. This quantum light energy can be in more than one place at any time. It travels instantly from one place to another. It can carry messages and is more powerful than anything man has created. This light energy shows how God is omnipotent, and continues to create the multi-verses.

At birth, we bring a Spirit/Soul into this world and it leaves when we pass on. Our Spirit/Soul is the image God gives us, but through free will, we can connect to God's Spirit during our lifetime or go our own way and disregard Him/Her. God constantly urges us to expand our spiritual horizons by metaphorically going through the Door that Jesus talked about in the Bible.

God is Alive and Well explores how the Creator can enrich our lives by helping us understand how He/She works with us and through us. This book shows us how all humans have a piece of God's Spirit in them – making us all brothers and sisters regardless of our race, culture, and religion. Not only are all humans connected to each other, we are also connected to the earth, which is part of the Light of God. *God is Alive and Well* brings us all together as one people, and one earth. Our relationship with each other and with the planet is the challenge God has for us today.

Chapter 1
Personal Beginning

As Charles Dickens wrote in *A Tale of Two Cities*, "It was the best of times, it was the worst of times." That sums up the era in which I was born in June of 1943—the middle of World War II. Although I can't prove it scientifically, in faith I believe that before we are born and still in Spirit, we decide what our life path and mission will be for this lifetime. We also select our earthly parents and family, as well as the precise time of our birth. If this is the case, why would anyone decide to be born in the middle of a war? Well, it turned out I was ahead of the curve of baby boomers who were born immediately after 1945, so I grew up in a period of shortages. My parents had just come through the Great Depression of the 1930s and had been severely damaged psychologically by that experience. Just prior to the Depression, my dad purchased the family farm in Southwestern Ontario, paying $6,000 for it. When the Depression hit, the mortgage on the farm might as well have been $6,000,000. My parents struggled to pay it, and most times could not. Fortunately, the mortgage wasn't held by the bank, but by a wealthy neighbor. He and my dad were both elders in the local Presbyterian church. I believe that without that connection, my family would have been homeless.

There was a "best of times" growing up on a farm in the 1940s and 50s, even though I didn't realize how poor we really were. Poverty is totally relevant to a person's situation. I knew we didn't have as much wealth as my cousin on the farm next to us, because he had a grain threshing machine and we didn't. He also had newer farm machinery and a newer car than we did. Everything we had was used and usually ten years old before my dad would even consider buying it, but these material things met our needs, so it didn't matter if they weren't to the same standard as our neighbors'. The low priority put on material things has had a major impact on how I value material goods to this day. As long as we had a roof over our heads, and food on the table, the rest of the material world would look after itself.

When I see parents today struggling to meet the needs of their children, whether it's registration fees for sports teams, dance clubs, or any other organized activity, I think of my own upbringing. During my childhood years, there were few to no clubs to join; even if there were any, we had no money to pay the membership fees. I must have had the most boring childhood possible. Not at all! I had freedom to come and go as I pleased. Activities and play became whatever I could create with my mind, and boy did I ever have a creative mind! Fortunately, my cousin, who was six months younger than me and lived on the next concession road, became my best friend. When we weren't in the one-room school house, we were together every chance we could get. Our games usually entailed a scenario of an episode of the *Lone Ranger*, which was highly popular at that time. Our weapons were usually made of something we'd crafted from wood, and the story always ended with the good guys winning over the fictitious bad guys.

The life of the local church provided moral guidance as I grew up. My father was the superintendent of the Sunday school, and skipping the weekly Sunday service was not an option. Learning the stories and creeds in the Bible was standard fare, and one did not question whether they were true or not, as it was never considered. I was told it was God's Word, and every word written was infallible. As I grew into my teenage years, the Young People's Society, a Christian group for teens, became my social outlet, and my belief system developed around the teachings and social interactions of the members. Moral standards of respect for yourself and others were totally ingrained and never questioned. That's not to say I didn't engage in what the church would term "sinful activities." Like all young people of every generation, I wasn't always the model son. My short temper was often the cause of my fall from grace, and it took many years to reign it in and accept it as the dark side of my character.

One of the greatest understandings I acquired growing up was that I was a "balanced person." The Christian church taught me about the evil, or sinful side of my character, and that it couldn't be tolerated in Christians. We were supposed to foster only the good in us and expunge the bad; however, that never made much sense to me. How can you get rid of a part of you and keep only the good part? I realized early in life that inside each of us is both good and evil. We can rise to the heights of a Mother Teresa or even Jesus Christ, but we also have within us the evil that can produce an Adolf Hitler. Many Christians don't want to acknowledge that weakness in their character, so they fight for their entire life to either get rid of it forever or bury it so deep that, hopefully, it will never surface. Often, I would see prominent people, such as ministers, rail against the sins of the flesh on Sunday morning and be caught visiting brothels during the week. The struggle to bury the dark side usually results in the light shining on the sinner for all to see. Naturally, as good Christians, we stand up in pontificated judgment on those who don't control their dark side. The prisons of Western society are full of those whose dark sides were exposed, as we have established laws to ensure they will not perpetrate their evil back in society; however, having studied and taught deviance and crime at the university level, I know that there are just as many people who have committed their evil in society but have never been exposed. Judgment is an issue to which I'll return as we examine the future of society.

Throughout my youth, my father wanted me to become a minister, but teaching children was my dream from a very early age. For nearly forty years I fulfilled that dream, and I hope I made a positive difference in the lives of the children I worked with during those years. Leadership was always a drawing card for me, and at the tender age of twenty-three, I became a school principal. Over the course of thirty-six years, I served as principal in eight schools in Ontario and Alberta, Canada. I can honestly say that children have had a greater effect on me than I had on them. The future of humankind rests with our children, and I have an optimistic hope for this earth and for the God who is alive and well and seeking an intimate relationship with each person. You'll be amazed how things can change when Holy Spirit power enters your life.

Chapter 2

A Soul's Awakening

What do we really mean by a "born again" or "soul awakening" experience? To explain it simply: you are turning your life over to God to lead you through this complex and often difficult three-dimensional life. In John 3:3, Jesus explains how we can become connected to God. Nicodemus, a member of the Jewish ruling council, asked Jesus how to do the miracles he saw Jesus perform. Jesus answered him: "Very truly I tell you, no one can see the Kingdom of God unless they are born again." The road map to living a "God inspired and guided life" doesn't seem to exist beyond being told to go and sin no more. Regretfully, we continue to struggle through life after our spiritual experience, and we wonder why our life didn't magically transform and become easier.

When we enter this life as a baby, we think of ourselves and those around us as made of flesh and blood in bodies that age, and we know that eventually we'll die. Since death is inevitable, we fight very hard to sustain this life as long as we possibly can, and to put off what we consider to be a dreadful end, which may lead to nothingness or to some place in the sky called heaven. We know that the body can't make it into heaven, so we develop a belief system that says we have a soul, or spirit, that survives us and goes to some sort of heavenly reward. How does our belief in a soul develop? Even though many people don't follow a particular religion, survival in the afterlife through the soul is a prominent belief throughout the world.

Have you ever questioned why you never seem to be quite satisfied with your life? You either look at the regrets of the past or make plans for the future that will produce better results. I was always seeking a better future. The old adage that the grass is always greener on the other side of the fence was certainly true for me, as it is for most people. Throughout our lifetime, we continually search for truth and our purpose for even being on this earth. The simple truth is that we aren't complete beings in body or soul until we seek a connection with the God who made us in His/Her image.

This truth leads us to seek out God. The religions that have developed in Western society follow the patriarch, Abraham, who fathered three religions: Christianity, Judaism, and Islam. These religions, through the Bible and other sacred texts, teach that God is an omnipotent being who sits in judgment over all mankind. He's considered patriarchal, and that masculine energy is predominant. To fully understand their teachings, the mind must be fully engaged, and precepts and laws must be fully adhered to. Any deviation results in sin, or worse, heresy, and laws that are broken must be judged and punishment meted out. As the religious teaching goes, sin can be forgiven, either directly by God or through a church leader such as a priest. The patriarchal system in the church spilled over into every aspect of life, such as politics and business, for thousands of years, eliminating half the population of the world—the females. Society's norms demanded that man exert exclusive control, leaving women on the fringes.

The teachings of Jesus in the New Testament totally challenged the patriarchal system of the religion of His day and continue to challenge our churches in the twenty-first century. Jesus spoke of loving your neighbor as you would love yourself. Does this sound like a patriarchal system to you? Jesus' teachings brought a balanced approach to living. He explained that you can't just live from your mind, but your heart must also be used when dealing with others in society.

To more fully understand the Jesus of the New Testament, we need to look to His Father/Mother God to understand who the Son was, but also who we are. To understand God, we have to understand that God is not a long-bearded, old man sitting in heaven on a throne, watching His creation and sending out orders to address the problems people pray to Him to solve. If God isn't in heaven, where is He? We need to look to recently discovered scientific research in quantum physics to fully understand the God of all creation. Scientists are in the beginning stages of measuring a new energy that many people over the centuries knew existed but couldn't prove. Some call this invisible energy *quantum energy*, *spiritual energy*, or *zero-point energy*. This energy can be in two places at the same time, has unlimited power, and can travel faster than the speed of light. This new-found energy is the God-energy of all creation in the universe; it not only created everything in this world, but continues to create even at this very moment. In a later chapter, we'll expand on God's relationship to us through this newly discovered energy in quantum physics, and I will try to keep it in layman's language.

God not only uses this energy to create, but He is of this energy Himself. The Bible states that God has always been, and this is true, as this spiritual energy has always existed. What we fail to realize is that God is using this spiritual energy to continually create Himself; as we explore our relationship to God, we come to see that we are part of God's continuing development. When God began His ascent into spirit at the beginning of time, He used the Word to begin His creation. In John 1:1, He states: "In the beginning was the Word, and the Word was with God, and the Word was God." Words are created from the mind. This began the patriarchal God that we see in the Old Testament. My theory is that over the eons of time, God realized He wasn't complete and balanced, and that He needed the heart to balance Himself. The creation story in Genesis describes Adam needing a mate to be complete, and how Eve was formed out of Adam's rib. This may be God's creation story of Himself, when He created the heart-essence out of His own energy to give Himself the balance He needed to be complete. Hence, we can refer to Father/Mother God as Creator of all that is.

Jesus came to this earth two thousand years ago to bring balance to humanity through His teachings. He showed mankind what a balanced, mind/heart, masculine/feminine person who is connected to God can do on earth. Not only did He preach love and kindness to all, but He healed sick people, restored limbs, and raised a man from the dead. Jesus set the pattern for all mankind to emulate as His followers; however, the religions of the world, steeped in the patriarchal system of thinking, intellectualized the teachings of Jesus rather than employing the heart to create the balanced God-person.

When I was growing up, my religion taught me to aspire to be like Jesus through service and right living. As far as Christ's miracles were concerned, they were part of the past and not part of life today. What always stuck in my mind was the question: Why not? When Jesus met His disciples just before He ascended into Heaven, He said, "Behold, everything I did you can do as well … and even more!" That told me that there was more to life than I'd been led to believe by my church. If Jesus' words were true, then the spark that we call our Soul/Spirit has a very important place in my future and the future of all mankind.

This leads us back to the place of men and women in our society today. As we have discussed, the masculine patriarchal systems have been the predominant energy for thousands of years. That is not to say that a few matriarchal societies haven't existed in history, but they are few and far between. The patriarchal societies have been based on masculine energy that is predominated by mind energy centered in the left brain. Its control is based on logical thinking driven by the five senses. Over the past three hundred years, scientists have based all their findings on Newtonian physics, which states that if you can't see it, it doesn't exist. This patriarchal approach left little to no room for the emotional, right brain approach to life. The right brain is associated with feminine energy. In effect, humankind accepted as truth only half of the human brain's guidance.

Let me clarify that God did not want humans to rely totally on masculine, left brain energy or feminine, right brain energy. He expected that every man and woman would contain both masculine and feminine energy, or mind and heart energy. He expected every human being to have a balance of both mind and heart. History has shown that relying solely on patriarchal energy has led us into centuries of wars as we competed for power over others or for scarce resources to sustain life.

When God created man and woman in the beginning, He saw the need for relationships. We are not solitary individuals, as stated in Genesis 2:24: "That is why a man leaves his father and mother and is united to his wife, and they became one flesh." God's plan was to unite the male and female so they would become one united and balanced family. Today, approximately half of all marriages split apart when they are no longer able to maintain the balanced energy of God. At the beginning of this message, we talked about how to create a spirit-filled person. Families must survive the multitude of challenges that come their way over years of marriage. The key to a lasting marriage is each person in the relationship awakening spiritually and connecting to God's Holy Spirit. Only with that connection can husbands and wives endure the challenges life throws at them over the years. I have always maintained that for a marriage to last, both partners must be whole, balanced individuals themselves. We often see two people come together expecting to join their two halves into one. In marriage, two halves do not make a whole. Only two people who are balanced in God's energy can make a whole, healthy marriage. God needs His followers to be balanced with both mind and heart, or masculine and feminine, energy. As the hymn goes, "We are one in the Spirit, we are one in the Lord, and we pray that all unity will one day be restored, and they'll know we are Christians by our love."

Chapter 3

Open My Eyes That I May See

*G*od sent His Holy Spirit that we may be able to see the Creator of the universe and all mankind. For forty days after His resurrection, Christ showed Himself to many of His followers, not only to show He was alive, but to continue to minister to them. Pentecost is one of the most amazing events to take place in the history of humankind. Let's look at this experience, which happened to not only Jesus' disciples, but to large gatherings of His followers who were hiding from the Roman soldiers who had recently killed their leader. There was much fear among the group, but also hope that their Savior was alive after being dead for three days. On the day of Pentecost, Jesus sent the promised Holy Spirit from God to help them live in connection to the Creator, Father/Mother. Acts 2:1–8, 11b–12 describes what happened.

> When the day of Pentecost came, they were all
> together in one place. Suddenly a sound like the

blowing of a violent wind came from heaven and filled the whole house where they were sitting. They saw what seemed to be tongues of fire that separated and came to rest on each of them. All of them were filled with the Holy Spirit and began to speak in other tongues as the Spirit enabled them. Now there were staying in Jerusalem God-fearing Jews from every nation under heaven. When they heard the sound, a crowd came together in bewilderment, because each one heard their own language being spoken. Utterly amazed, they asked: "Aren't all these who are speaking Galileans? Then how is it that each of us hears them in our native language? …We hear them declaring the wonders of God in our own tongues!" Amazed and perplexed they asked one another, "What does this mean?"

Acts 2 goes on to state that not everyone experienced this phenomenon, and some made the accusation that those speaking in tongues were drunk, but Peter addressed them to refute this. He explained that Jesus was just fulfilling His promise to send a Helper from God. It obviously worked, as we've seen Christians following this Holy Spirit for over two thousand years; however, God and Jesus detractors have also been around for the same two thousand years. It's as if a film has been placed over the eyes of the people of the world for millennia.

Today, God wants us to shed the misinformation that has grown up outside and inside Christianity. God is alive and well and is sending His Holy Spirit once again, as strongly as He did at that first Pentecost. God wants us to see Him more clearly than at any other time in history. In the Old Testament, God met with leaders like Moses and the prophets, who tried to help the people of Israel through the establishing of the Law. Unfortunately, their words usually fell on deaf ears, and the result was disaster for them. They were conquered and sent off to slavery in the victor's country.

God is a very patient Spirit, so He tried a different approach in the New Testament by sending Jesus to the earth to more directly influence not only the Jewish people, but over time all the people of the world, the Gentiles. God thought that the people who were open to religious ideas would listen to Jesus, who ministered to them and taught about how to live a righteous life. He also believed people would pay closer attention to His words if He showed the power of God through amazing miracles. The people who followed Jesus believed He would be the king who would free them from slavery to Rome, but Jesus never sought to be a physical king. He is a spiritual king.

For two thousand years, Christians have followed Jesus' teachings, which set a very high standard for living, as did the Old Testament laws. Over time, though, Christ's miracles got lost in Christianity. Jesus told His followers that they could do the same miracles He did, and even more (Mark 16)! As we look over the past two thousand years, we see great emphasis placed on what Jesus taught, and we marvel at the miracles He performed, but we're still looking for King Jesus to return to become the earthly king the disciples wanted in the first place. We still believe He will return when the time is right, but we've failed to fulfill the one commission He gave us, which is to connect to God and use the Holy Spirit in our lives to become the leaders of the world He asked us to be.

In the beginning, God created man out of the dust of the ground, but as we know now from quantum mechanics, even the dust is really compacted light particles from the God-energy. When woman was created, the rib of Adam was used. Logically speaking, God created women with the same Creator-energy He used to create man. When we think of humankind as made in the image of God, we realize that we may be more God-like than anyone could have imagined. Our bodies are an incredible mastery of design, and God is the master physicist and mathematician.

In recent years, there has been a major push to clone animals. Some people talk of eventually cloning humans, but I don't think we have to fear that we'll ever see that happen. Those who would seek to do exactly what God has done fail to see the magnificence of the Creator. We sometimes think we know as much as God and that we are our own creators. When we think we know more than Him, we need to remember what God said to Job in Job 42.

Most people live their lives struggling to find out who they are when the answer is really inside of them. God gave us an eternal Spirit/Soul to guide us though our lifetime(s). We are motivated to search for satisfaction in our lives because Jesus continually knocks at our Spirit/Soul's door, telling us there is a better way to live. Sadly, we run into a problem, much like the light switch that is turned to the off position. We live in the darkness, not realizing that we need to turn on the light switch so we can finally see. Without that switch turned on, we can't see reality or what is going on around us. We're like a blind person groping around in the dark; after a while, we lose sight of reality altogether. For eons, God has tried to heal our metaphoric blindness. When we open the pure connection with God through our own Spirit/Soul, we can see the world and people around us in a true spiritual light. It becomes impossible for the world's lies to lead us off the narrow path that God has in mind for us.

Humanity is also attempting to create robots to do what we have done for millennia. The ultimate aim is to create a robot that looks and acts as we do, possibly with super-human applications. The fear is that robots will become superior to us, and we'll become irrelevant. Let me assure you that this can never happen. People who connect to God through their Spirit/Soul are the real super-humans, and no matter how hard technologists try, they can never duplicate God's creation.

Science is making major strides in understanding the human body through DNA analysis and manipulation of the genome; however, they have a long way to go to understand the functions of our DNA. At this point, approximately 3 percent of the double helix is understood. That means we're still learning about the other 97 percent of the functions of our DNA. Scientists are beginning to believe that God's energy may be what resides in the 97 percent that has been called "junk." They're feverously working to understand how DNA functions and to develop instruments that can view quantum particles of light, which may eventually show the Creative God-energy.

Let's look at how the God-energy functions in the human body. What we see is a physical body that has five senses to guide it from infancy through to old age and death, as long as it isn't interrupted prematurely by disease, accident, or some other life-ending situation. Our human bodies function consciously and unconsciously. There are functions in our bodies that we direct consciously, such as our plans and instructions for our bodies to carry out. We also function on the auto-pilot of our unconscious body, such as when our hearts beat, when we breathe, or when our digestive system takes in and digests food and drink. God set up a very fine balance in our physical bodies, but due to unforeseen invasions, disease can cause physical parts to fail.

For most of our lives, we've used chemicals created by the pharmaceutical industry to alleviate the pain and suffering, but as you may have noticed, the actual problem isn't fixed. Think of the billions of dollars that have been raised and spent on the cancer epidemic. When I think of my late wife's brain cancer, I just don't see any change in the number of people being totally healed of that dreaded disease. Today, we are still resorting to surgery, radiation, and chemotherapy to stop the cancer. After my wife was diagnosed with a brain tumor the size of a grapefruit, the doctors performed surgery to remove it. Amazingly, my wife seemed fine and was able to function normally; however, the doctors decided to make sure they got all of the tumor by using radiation to kill what may have been missed in the operation. During this treatment, my wife, who was a fluent reader and could type two hundred words per minute, began to lose her ability even to read, let alone type anything. I tried to work with her to help her learn to read again, but the efforts were futile. She wasn't subjected to chemotherapy, as that treatment came along after her death.

Chemotherapy is the use of poisonous chemicals designed to kill the cancer cells, but the unfortunate side effect is the destruction of good cells as well as the immune system that God gave us to ward off disease in the first place. Many people have endured chemotherapy in order to live longer, and I'd never take that away from anybody. My concern is that our approach to healing that disease, and other failures in the human body, is contrary to how God made us in the first place. Simply put, we're trying to solve our physical problems with a chemical process when the problems need an energy response. Our bodies are made of energy in the solid form of captured God-energy. That's not to say that some forms of illness don't respond to chemicals, but most of our illnesses need a spiritual answer, in keeping with the way we were created.

The other issue that science and the pharmaceutical industry have done an even less stellar job in dealing with is the problem of our emotional and mental bodies. First of all, humankind comes at most problems from a left-brain approach. The left side of our brain controls logical thinking. Reading and mathematics are functions of the left brain. Most problems in society continue to be solved using left brain thinking. If you're looking for your ego, you'll find him working out of the left side of the brain. The problem with this approach is that we ignore the other half of our brain. So what's so important about the right side of the brain? Your emotions reside in this portion. The right side of your brain controls the aesthetics of your life. Music and drama and all creativity come out of this part. Many people listen to music on their technological devices to balance their lives, especially when their work draws mainly on the left brain.

The emotional body is just as susceptible to dark energy in the form of anger, hatred, division, and lies. This energy is stored in our emotional bodies, just as illness and disease collects in the physical body. The emotional body responds to what we see, and it automatically stores those images as energy. We can't see them physically, but they come back to us in our dreams and as memories of horrific events in our lives. The most dramatic ones that come back to haunt us are images seen in war on the battlefield. We call it PTSD, but it's really energy that our emotional body stores up, no matter how hard we try to bury or get rid of it. We also see this energy in road rage, which is triggered by another dark issue in life that causes the person to lose all sense of reality and commit crimes they would never think of doing in normal situations.

Depression occurs when the emotional body becomes so full of negative or imbalanced energy that life feels futile. Often when one more piece of imbalanced energy hits, all hope is lost, and suicide seems the only option. The pharmaceutical industry tries to solve the emotional problems of people with drugs that have short term solutions but fail to address the need for balanced energy. The solution is to spiritually clear out the negative, imbalanced energy and draw in the balanced light energy of the Creator God-energy. Once again, the answer is in accepting the connection between God and our own Spirit/Soul.

The second part of our body that seems to be totally overlooked by the scientific community is the mental body. What is our mental body? Simply put, it is our belief system. Social science has tried to make sense of why we believe as we do and why we act as we do. We are born into families that live in a particular culture with linguistic uniqueness. Throughout our life, we tend to stay within that culture group, because we're most comfortable being around people we know and like, and who think the way we do. The more isolated we are from other groups that are dissimilar to us, the less likely we are to adopt other groups' views. We come to tolerate our own people and distrust anyone different from us.

Over our lifetime, we develop beliefs in our mental bodies that support who we are and negate people who are different or have views that are not part of our group's beliefs. Negative beliefs that we consider normal are really imbalanced energy, which is contrary to what God has taught us through prophets and teachers like Jesus. As a result, even people who claim to follow Christian principles are overshadowed by the imbalanced beliefs held in the mental body. Interestingly, imbalanced energy in the mental body often moves out and changes when we move outside our culture group. We see this when young people go to college or university and meet people from other cultural and religious groups who seem to be just like them. For centuries, God has taught that humankind is the same, no matter what their belief systems are or what religion they follow. All are part of God's Kingdom, and one person isn't greater than another. We are all equal in God's sight, no matter how much we try to make our group or ourselves better that anyone else.

Once again, our belief systems in our mental bodies are filled with balanced and imbalanced energy, but not all imbalanced energy is bad. The rule to follow is the belief system that one holds regarding God's teachings. There are times in our lives that Jesus knocks at our spiritual door, and the Holy Spirit comes into our lives and helps us clean out the imbalanced belief systems we have collected. God will always give you a choice as to whether you want to keep that imbalanced energy or let it go. Free choice is the gift God has given us. God may knock at your door many times in your lifetime, but it's entirely up to you whether you want to connect to Him or go your own way and live your life as you see fit. God will not judge you for not letting Him into your life. He/She will just look at you and say, "Maybe next time."

Chapter 4
The Energy of God

How do we know and understand who God is if we continue, as Christians, to think of Him/Her as some higher source that exists outside of us and reminds us of a white-bearded grandfather sitting on a celestial throne and giving directions to the angels, judging the actions of humans, and answering prayers? Unfortunately, the image, or persona, we have of Creator God seems to have been warped over time. Our Judeo-Christian upbringing puts God at a distance, and it's up to us to search for Him/Her throughout our lifetime … often with little success. Our religions tend to set an intermediary between us and God. The intermediary may be a priest or prophet whom we must approach to seek God on our behalf. In the Christian churches, Jesus is our intermediary. Our belief system teaches us that we are unworthy to approach God directly, as we will burn up and be destroyed in His/Her intensity. Moses learned this on the Mount when he received the Ten Commandments (Exodus 19:21). If God is so powerful, of what is He/She composed? Energy! Yes, spiritual energy. What we've never fully understood is how God functions as the Creator.

Let's take a moment and think of our three-dimensional world. It's governed by our five senses, and scientists believe that if something can't be seen and empirically proven, then it just doesn't exist. However, our physics researchers are greatly changing their theories. A century ago, Albert Einstein and a group of researchers speculated that there is energy affecting the earth, but we can't see it with the naked eye or even with a high-power microscope. The study of this mysterious energy is called quantum physics, and research into its attributes has been going on for the past one hundred years. Some of the amazing things physicists have discovered are that this energy, when projected, can be in two places at the same time; it's not governed by the speed of light (186,000 miles per second); and it has a power that far exceeds anything we know of on earth. Scientists continue to research this quantum energy, and the rush is on to see it through specialized microscopes to determine its properties. What scientists aren't saying is that this is the God-energy that created the universe and everything in it through exquisite design. If that is the case, then we, as humans, are part of that great design, and the Genesis story of creation may be less of a fairy tale than we realize. We are created in the image of God for a very divine purpose on this earth.

The Bible is filled with examples of how this divine energy brought about what we consider to be miracles. How do we explain stories that we read in both the Old and New Testament that seem to defy logic? My Christian upbringing taught me that those things could happen two or three thousand years ago, but not in this day and age. Well, spiritual energy isn't something that can just disappear if the Creator God used it to create the universe, and specifically earth and all life on it. Let's take a moment and think about what stories in the Old Testament directly demonstrate that God's energy was definitely active.

Most Christians know the story of Moses, the adopted son of the daughter of the Egyptian Pharaoh. As a young man, Moses tried to defend a fellow Israelite who was being beaten by an Egyptian taskmaster. Moses committed murder and fled for his life into the desert, where he spent approximately sixty years as a shepherd. He was married and had children. What we aren't given are details of his life during that period of time. All we can surmise is that it was a preparation for the third segment of his life. His life in the desert took a strange turn of events when he was visited by an angel in a burning bush, which in reality was a heavenly vision directing him to return to Egypt to free his people from slavery. Moses showed his vulnerable human side when he expressed fear for his life if he returned to face those who wanted him dead. God told him that Aaron, his older brother, would be his spokesman.

At this point in the story, I'd ask if Moses comes across to you as someone who was greater in some ways than the average person. The answer is obviously NO! So what made Moses seem to be more than a man when he reached Egypt and started demanding the release of his people, the Israelites, by performing miracles? First of all, the Bible says that God was in direct communication with Moses. He picked up God's instructions on how the miracles were to be carried out. Exodus 7:10 to Exodus 11:5 outlines the ten miracles Moses rained down on Egypt. The first three miracles—wooden rods becoming serpents, the Nile River turning to blood, and millions of frogs invading the land— were miracles the Egyptian magicians were able to do, illustrating that these miracles were not just from God but could be replicated by other humans. This raises the question of where the magicians got their access to what can only be described as spiritual creation energy. The remaining seven miracles were limited to Moses' power: the lice infestation, the swarms of flies, the death of Egyptian animals, the painful boils, the hail, the rain and thunder, the millions of locusts sent to devour everything left after the other pestilences, the complete darkness for three days, and finally the death of all first-born children of the Egyptians. How could an ordinary man become a super-human who could do God's bidding by performing miracles by just stretching out his shepherd's staff and verbally calling down plagues on the Egyptians? This question stuck with me for years as a follower of Christ.

The miracle of the parting of the Red Sea also fascinated me, especially when I saw Charlton Heston in the movie *The Ten Commandments* hold out that staff and command the Red Sea to part so the Israelites could walk across on dry ground (Exodus 14:21–22). Obviously, an ordinary man couldn't do what Moses did.

If we look at this scenario from a spiritual perspective, the burning bush represents Jesus' door in the spiritual awakening. From that moment on, Moses walked on the spiritual side of the door. He was now totally connected to his own Spirit/Soul, which gave him a direct connection with the Creator God. Not only that, but Moses also had access to the creative energy of God, which allowed him to perform unheard of miracles that went far beyond the limited energy ability of Pharaoh's magicians. The spiritual energy of God is the same energy that created everything that exists on earth. Most religions believe God performed the miracles, but if you read the biblical texts carefully, you'll see it was God telling Moses to perform the miracles. It definitely raises serious questions for the average human about what the true capabilities are for those who pass through the door that Jesus invites us to enter.

The Old Testament also illustrates the spiritual energy of God through two prophets, Elijah and Elisha. We sometimes forget the miracles these two men performed. Were they ordinary human beings? YES! Elijah feared for his life for many years as the King of Israel's wife, Jezebel, sought to kill him. He had to hide and use his spiritual powers to keep from being found. Elijah revealed his ability to use the spiritual creative energy of God to create meal and cooking oil that never depleted for a widow and her son (1 Kings 17:14), because she had befriended him and fed him her last bit of food rather that keeping it for herself and her son. The scripture doesn't indicate that Elijah was told by God to do this, as in the case of Moses. Obviously, Elijah understood the creative power of Creator God and used it to create food and oil for the woman and her son, in much the same manner as the manna was brought down to earth to feed the people of Israel for forty years in the desert.

Elijah, like Jesus, raised someone from the dead. The widow's son died, and Elijah prayed for life to return to the boy. He stretched out on top of the boy three times, and the boy came back to life (1 Kings 18:43–45). Once again, we see the spiritual energy of God at work, performing a miracle to bring life to a child who had been dead for a few days. The Prophet Elisha, Elijah's student, performed the same miracle on the Shunammite's son, who had also died. Elisha was summoned by the mother, who believed he could also perform the miracle of bringing someone back from the dead. Elisha put his mouth over the dead boy's mouth and also stretched himself out on top of the boy, calling him to come back to life. Elisha did this seven times, and at that point the child came back to life. Only the spiritual energy of Creator God can give life, but these scriptures show that a human who has crossed through the door into spirituality has access to that spiritual energy—a gift to mankind from God.

Elijah provides further examples of how the spiritual energy works. Because of the sins of the people of Israel, Elijah pronounced in the name of the Lord that no rain would fall for three years. Did Elijah have the power over the weather, or was that God doing it (1 Kings 17:14)? The answer to that question is found in 1 Kings 18:43–45, when Elijah calls for the rain to come again after the three years of drought. From scripture, it's quite apparent that Elijah is calling on the spiritual energy to bring a downpour. Prior to this, Elijah had proven to King Ahab and the prophets of Baal whose power was greatest. Both the prophets of Baal and Elijah built altars to sacrifice to their god or Creator God. The catch was that neither could use anything to start the fire in the wood. The prophets of Baal prayed for fire to come down and set the wood on fire and burn their sacrifice all day, but with no success. Then Elijah soaked the wood under his sacrifice with six barrels of water. Next, he called for fire to come down from heaven, and it did—consuming everything. This was Elijah's way of proving that the spiritual energy of God had no equal in those Old Testament days, and it has that same power today.

Finally, Elijah gave us one more miracle that takes the spiritual energy to a whole new level of understanding. When Elijah decided that the end of his life was near and it was time to return to the spiritual realm, or heaven, he did not die! Unlike Jesus, who died, came back to life, and then rose into heaven by what we call the resurrection, Elijah translated into pure light and was taken into heaven. Elisha, who witnessed the event, said that Elijah rode in something that was like a chariot of light (2 Kings 2:12). This was the ultimate power of the spiritual energy of God. There is a side note to this amazing story: Elijah promised his student, Elisha, that if he witnessed him being taken into heaven, he would receive the mantle, or spiritual tools, Elijah had to carry on his work. We know it worked, because we see Elisha smiting the River Jordan with his staff. The river divided, allowing passage across on the dry river bed. Previously, we discussed Elisha's raising of the Shunammite boy.

We need to ask what these Old Testament miracles mean for us personally. The Christian churches have for centuries taught that the miracles of the Bible were performed by God, who intervened personally for whatever reason to change the course of history for people. However, when God created humans, He gave us free will to live our lives as we determine. How can Creator God be both an advocate for free will and at the same time set up interference in people's lives? The answer must be in the people who performed the miracles with God's help, which raises another question: Who are the individuals God trusts to bestow these gifts on, and how do they get to that relationship with God?

This brings us to the New Testament with its core focus on one man, Jesus. For two thousand years, biblical scholars

and average people, like you and me, have struggled to understand who Jesus really was and why He even came to this
earth. The one thing we can all agree on is that this one man
changed the course of world history for the past two millennia. Christianity in its many forms has shaped religious
beliefs and practices—in some cases not for the best, when
we consider the Crusades of the Dark Ages and the number
of wars fought in His name. But who was Jesus? Everyone
seems to agree that He was a human being who was born
as a baby, even if it was by a mysterious virgin birth. I won't
get into whether a miracle virgin birth can happen, but it
may not be as farfetched as it seems. Life in spirituality offers
human beings great ability when they step through the door
to fully embrace the world of God.

We know that even before Jesus began His ministry, He
was tempted by the dark side, which is represented by the
devil in Matthew 4:3–10. Three times he was tempted to not
cross over to God's side of the door, but He responded with,
"Man shall not live by bread alone, but by every word that
proceeds out of the mouth of God." Jesus was saying that
mankind must look beyond the material life to focus on what
God's message gives each of us to guide us in our daily living.

Jesus also showed Himself to be a man when he was
baptised by John the Baptist, just like any other human. The
only difference was that Jesus showed us the door into the
spiritual life at the moment the Spirit of God descended on
Him in the form of a dove. From that time on, Jesus began

a ministry to the people. Many of His life lessons are well known to those who have spent time in Christian churches, as they pertain to living a righteous life in relation to other people. The biggest challenge Christians face is trying to follow the path Jesus taught.

Falling off the wagon of Christian living has become big business for religion, as the church tries to help people clear away the "sin" so they can get back on the righteous path once again. Some religions formalized the process so that the sinner could confess to a priest to intervene on his/her behalf and then do some penitence to get right with God. This put power in the hands of the few individuals who could forgive transgressions on behalf of God. In this system, mankind doesn't have to face God by himself/herself, as someone else looks after their "sins."

Jesus never taught that a mediator was needed to communicate with God personally. Sin wasn't even a topic He discussed, but after His death and resurrection, prophets such as Paul began to preach that Jesus died for the sins of mankind so that we could finally get right with God (1 Corinthians 15:3, Galatians 1:4, Romans 5:8). The problem is that Jesus has become the mediator of our tendency to fall off the righteous road He taught us to follow. According to the ancient prophets, right down to the present-day Christian church, we are all life failures and sinners. We were all born this way, and we all need saving. Supposedly Jesus can do that for us as the mediator between us and a vengeful God, who expects perfection from us.

It seems that we are caught between a rock and a hard place with no means of redemption, because we just can't seem to get our act together and live a proper life following the principles Jesus taught. Did you ever wonder why God would set up such a scenario for mankind when He knew we just couldn't live up to those high expectations? We spend a lifetime living in fear of failing God and not making it into heaven when we finally pack off this world at the end of our earthly existence.

What a sad commentary for a world of humans who believe in God but can't seem to follow very simple ways of creating positive relationships with those around us. Instead, we constantly judge others for their failures without even thinking. Rather than accepting others for who they are, we treat them harshly and with unacceptance. We even carry out hurtful acts to show others we are somehow superior to them. As a teacher of social psychology, I believe other people who come into our lives mirror back to us things we need to address in ourselves. Just think of people who have been married and divorced and then choose new mates with many of the same personality traits as the first spouse. Obviously, something is wrong when we seem to keep falling back into old patterns of beliefs and habits. The answer is staring us in the face, and that answer is Jesus. Why have we deified Jesus to the point that we can no longer see what He was really trying to show us?

Chapter 5

Who Are We in God's Eyes?

We often believe that God sees us as physical, flesh and blood beings; however, if we're made in God's image, then this perception of how God relates to us is a little skewed. Let's take a moment and revisit the God-energy, or the energy of quantum physics. Science has proven that everything is made up of atoms that we can see with specialized microscopes. There are smaller units of matter, but let's just deal at the atomic level for this discussion. The atom is a basic unit of matter that consists of a dense central nucleus surrounded by a cloud of negatively charged electrons. The atomic nucleus contains a mix of positively charged protons and electrically neutral neutrons. To simplify this— EVERYTHING IS ENERGY. Quantum physicists discovered that physical atoms are made up of vortices of energy that are constantly spinning and vibrating, like a spinning top that radiates unique energy signatures. Albert Einstein recognized that energy and matter are one and the same when he concluded that $E = MC^2$, which means that: E (ENERGY) = M (MATTER/MASS) x (times) C^2 (SPEED OF LIGHT (186,000 miles per second) (SQUARED).

The cells in our body—all fifty trillion of them—are made up of those spinning atoms. Although you cannot see it, you are a total energy being. What makes our human bodies so unique is that every cell in our body has a specific job. Some are blood cells, others are immune cells that fight off diseases, and others are heart cells, liver cells, brain cells, bone cells, and skin cells … to name just a few. Think of how amazing our bodies are. Only God could design something as miraculous as that, and He does that perfect job for us in the womb all the way through our life. It boggles my mind that our bodies are like factory workers building the most exquisite machine. As an aside, the image of humans as a machine is one in which the medical industry in Western countries believes strongly. Whenever any part of our body malfunctions, it's up to the pharmaceutical industry to fix the problem with a chemical concoction. What is missing from the equation is how God put us together in the first place—as energy beings. Biologists have recently discovered that we don't just have one brain, but that the membrane of every cell is a mem-brain. You thought we had challenges dealing with our one brain, but every cell in our body has the capacity to accept messages and send them as well. Just think of how fast that pain travels through your body when you stub your toe.

Let's look at the master-controlling brain. Our brains function on a CONSCIOUS and SUBCONSCIOUS level. The conscious brain functions for present thinking; the subconscious brain functions are on autopilot and control learned behaviors and memories. If this isn't complicated enough, let's look at who we really are. As bodies of energy, we aren't just one body, but FOUR! When we think of our four bodies, it makes total sense. We have a PHYSICAL body, which reacts and controls our five senses. We also have an EMOTIONAL body, a MENTAL body, and a SPIRIT/ SOUL body. We can't see three of the four bodies, but each has a major influence on the physical body. Since we are energy, it's only natural that energy outside of our bodies can have positive or negative effects on any or all of the four bodies. In a perfect state of being, our connectedness to God can lead to a BALANCED human. This means that God's Light fills all four of our bodies. When our bodies become IMBALANCED, with what the church calls "sins' and others call "dark energy," our bodies begin to fail.

Let's look at how imbalanced energy in each of the four bodies can have a detrimental effect on us. In the physical body, imbalanced energy from extreme stress or environmental issues, over time, can result in headaches, high blood pressure, heart palpitations, muscle tension, heavy breathing, disturbed sleep, loss of appetite, nausea, dry mouth, gastritis, ulcers, irritable bowel syndrome, backache, excessive sweating, rashes, acne, hives, and other illnesses or diseases.

In the emotional body, imbalanced energy from repressed, denied, or ignored emotions can, over time, result in hatred, envy, jealousy, and other destructive attitudes and feelings that manifest in the body. In time, you could develop a stiff shoulder, a sluggish liver, cancer, or other illnesses.

In the mental body, imbalanced energy from belief systems that are closed or genetic will say: "I know I'll get this illness, because my mother had it and so did my grandmother." The body hears and responds to your thoughts, beliefs, and words. Our Spirit/Soul can also have imbalanced energy from denying of Creator God in our lives. Spirit is not a partner in our lives. Unresolved karma can also result in imbalance in our Spirit/Soul. This can have a devastating effect, as it impacts all four of our bodies.

Imbalances in body, mind, and emotions set the stage for us to become victims of our environment as opposed to active partners in influencing our environment. Imbalanced energy is a challenge for all of us. If we want a total connection to God, who supplies us with positive, spiritual, balanced energy, our challenge is to move out the imbalanced energy and seek God to fill us. So how do we connect with God to do this?

- Our CELLS contain the imbalanced energy from our physical, emotional, mental, and Spirit/Soul bodies, which impacts our health and wellness.

- Our CELLS know the imbalanced, as well as the balanced, energy in them. Remember, each has a BRAIN.
- When called upon, the CELLS will move out the imbalanced energy and receive balanced energy from the Lord, restoring health and wellness.

What does a balanced person look like?
- has excellent health and lives much longer
- is gentle, patient, and slow to anger
- does not have to prove themselves to others
- will not push themselves and their thoughts on others
- will be sought out by others because of their balanced energy

Chapter 6

From Christianity to Spirituality

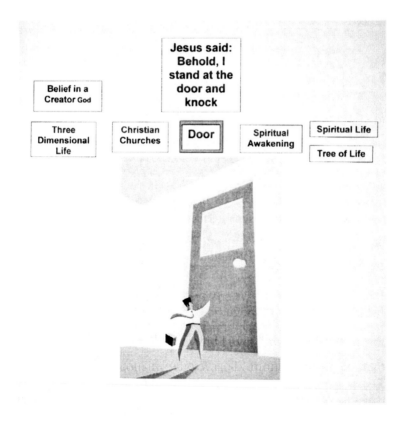

*B*ehold, I stand at the door, and knock: if any man hear my voice, and open the door, I will come in to him, and will sup with him, and he with me. To him that overcometh will I grant to sit with me in my throne, even as I also overcame, and am set down with my Father in his throne. (Revelation 3:20–22, KJV).

To him that overcometh will I give to eat of the tree of life, which is in the midst of the paradise of God. (Revelation 2:7, KJV).

I think that the greatest challenge faced by a person following Christian teachings and traditions is to follow Jesus through the doorway into the spiritual life. Many Christians come to believe that the doorway to God can only be crossed by the physical body's death. Jesus didn't teach us that we had to die to find a life in the Spirit. He simply said: "Ask, and it shall be given you; seek, and you shall find; knock, and it shall be opened unto you: For everyone that asketh receiveth; and to him that knocketh it shall be opened" (Mathew 7:7–8, KJV).

What does it mean to walk through the door that Jesus indicates is necessary if we wish to follow Him? We must first step back and examine who we are at the moment we make the decision to walk through a spiritual door into a new and challenging realm that promises us we can return to Creator God if we follow this teaching. However, it isn't as simple as it may sound. Anyone should be able to walk through an invisible door to which Jesus holds the key. The Christian religions of the world teach us that we only have one shot at this, and if we fail, our sin will preclude us from getting into heaven. We may even have to spend some of our eternity in purgatory, or be outright rejected and spend the rest of eternity in the fires of hell.

Christian churches don't teach that our Spirits may not be on earth for the first time, even though reincarnation was part of the belief system in biblical times. In Matthew 16:13, Jesus asked his disciples: "'Who do people say the Son of Man is?' They replied, 'Some say John the Baptist; others say Elijah; and still others, Jeremiah or one of the prophets.'" The early Christian church needed some way of maintaining power over its adherents. If people thought they had more than one shot at redemption, with more than one lifetime to get it right, the church hierarchy would lose its power over the masses. We must remember that religious teachings came totally by word of mouth, and it wasn't until the Middle Ages with the invention of the Guttenberg printing press that the written word in the Bible could be read by the educated people, who were few in number up until the twentieth century.

The teachings of the Bible became well entrenched in the Christian churches. Unfortunately, the teachings of Jesus became lessons for the mind, and Jesus' teachings of the heart were downplayed. Mysticism grew up around the man, Jesus, who came to this earth as the Son of God to show through both the mind and the heart how everyone can return back to Creator God, from whom all have come. We have become so caught up in His virgin birth, His death on the cross, and His resurrection after three days, that we have lost the vision of who Jesus really was. Jesus was a "way-shower" who came to this earth as God's messenger to show everyone how to return home to God. We think of the Sermon on the Mount as one of the most profound messages ever given, and we analyze its meaning for our own lives. What we fail to understand is that Jesus was telling us we need to become balanced individuals who are both mind and heart conscious. The message in Mathew 5:3–11 begins with the word "Blessed" and shows how the spiritual person must live his/her life after accepting Jesus' invitation to walk through that door.

Jesus also showed how a balanced person living the spiritual life must approach others who need healing and help. Some Christian churches preach that, with prayer, miracles can happen today, but not often. As soon as we remove God and Jesus from ourselves and expect miracles, such as physical healings, to occur, we remove our own Spirit/Soul from the equation, failing to accept our personal responsibility in aiding that person's healing. As we examine life on the other side of the spiritual door later in this book, we'll see our place in this miracle of life.

The Challenge of Walking through the Door

When we come into this world as a baby and grow to maturity through to old age, we feel alone. We believe our life is a competition, whether for survival, jobs, or mates. Most of us, both male and female, believe we are alone, and that in order to "get ahead," we must use our minds and compete with others for those scarce resources. The heart is reserved for people we consider special in our lives, such as family and loved ones. Even these may not be granted full heart love, depending on how we feel we have been treated by them.

The problem with this thinking is that Creator God may have blinded us to our true connection to each other so that we can play out our life games on this earth. What religion fails to teach us is that we're far more connected to each other than most of us realize. First of all, let's look at our connection to God. Each of us has a Soul/Spirit that comes directly from God. We call Him/Her our Father/Mother. That denotes family. We're not only a part of the family of God, but we are His/Her sons and daughters. If we are sons and daughters of God, doesn't that make Jesus our brother? Since God is Spirit, He/She has a direct connection to our Soul/Spirit. God's connection to us is through what has often been referred to as an invisible cord. If we're that closely connected to God and are a piece of God, you'd think we would know it.

Unfortunately, until you open the Door that Jesus referred to and enter the spiritual life, you do not have a connection to your own Spirit. The access to your own Soul/Spirit has been lost since the beginning of time, all the way back to Adam and Eve's departure from the Garden of Eden, the location of the Tree of Life. The tree still exists on the other side of the door. Walking through the door gives you access to your own Soul/Spirit, and in turn to not only God, but to all those whom you have known and are now on the spiritual side themselves. This is often referred to as the veil between our three-dimensional world, or the world of the "afterlife."

While we're in this world, we think we're independent individuals and not connected to anyone else. God maintains a connection to us through the cord of the Spirit, and what we fail to realize is that every relationship we create with other human beings also sets up that spiritual cord. The cord connects our Soul/Spirit with his or her Soul/Spirit. Often these relationships are long term, lasting for eons of time in various lifetimes. Other times they are brief relationships that exist more as acquaintances. Some relationships that have existed for a long time will have a cord that appears more like a rope, while other short-term relationships may be barely a thread.

All our Souls/Spirits are connected, because we are all part of the Creator God. When we look around the world, we question how people who are part of the same Creator God can act so treacherously toward others, and sometimes even within their own families. The answer is simple: they have not walked through Jesus' door to a balanced life of mind and heart. Various religious groups believe that people who don't believe as they do are rejected by God and must be cast out or even killed. Most religions are ruled by the mind and are very paternal in their approach to their adherents, but Jesus didn't preach vengeance on those who were against Him. Instead, He preached forgiveness and "turning the other cheek."

Walking through the door isn't as easy as it sounds, but the rewards on the other side are so phenomenal that you don't want to turn back once you've experienced spiritual life. Many "born again" or "spiritually awakened" people expect a major change in their lives. Everything should get easier, right? Unfortunately, quite often the opposite is true, and life gets tougher. What we don't realize is that walking through the door does not mean that we leave our previous life and habits behind. The act of walking through the door into the spiritual life is a commitment on our part to live in a state of being where we want to be personally connected to our own Soul/Spirit and be in a direct connection with our Creator God.

Initially, some individuals receive what I call the "Damascus experience" that the Apostle Paul had, with visions of intense light and messages from Jesus, spiritual masters, or from God Himself/Herself. This was my own personal experience when I walked through the door into the spiritual life. Other people have a quiet entry with little fanfare, but with a beautiful, loving feeling that can only be described as God's incredible love for us. Walking through the door is just the beginning. Every person experiences it in his/her own way, as everyone walks a unique path back to God.

As I've already stated, walking through the door to the spiritual life isn't as easy as it sounds. Unfortunately, we don't leave our baggage from our previous life at the door. Just because we walk through a door doesn't mean we start over from scratch. We may intend to advance our life by seeking to reconnect with our Soul/Spirit, but we still have our former life issues to deal with beyond the door. It's the old issues that we played out in karmic situations in this life or previous lifetimes that become roadblocks to living the new spiritual life while still on this earth. Our former three-dimensional life wasn't a balanced life situation. Most actions came through the mind or through the heart, which supports our emotions. Our actions were often not rooted in right mindedness, but in our ego. The ego is prominent in the three-dimensional world, but must take a backseat when we cross through the door into the spiritual life. The ego becomes a hindrance when you move into the balanced life of Spirit. How do you shut down the dominance of your ego? You begin by dealing with the imbalances created by the ego prior to your entry into the spiritual life.

Imbalances influence our psyches, causing us to feel like we're victors over others, or victims of relationships with others. Both perceptions put us at the mercy of our personal belief systems. The balanced person, as he/she grows in the spiritual life, feels peace towards others and doesn't allow himself/herself to feel victimization or victorious. How can we deal with the issues that hold us back after we've crossed the threshold to the new life? Communication with those who have victimized you or whom you have victimized is crucial if you wish to move ahead. If at all possible, a face-to-face meeting is ideal, with a sincere apology for any wrongdoing to that person. This is an extremely challenging thing to do, but if you don't do it, this fractured relationship will act like a ball and chain around you and will continually pull you back through the door to your previous life. If you're unable to reconcile with the other person in a face-to-face meeting, a telephone call or written message may suffice to return the relationship to a neutral position.

I've also discussed the cord. We're all connected with others throughout this life and are reconnected with others from previous lifetimes. Our three-dimensional lives are a series of life learning experiences. We decide how we'll live our life prior to our birth while still on the other side of the spiritual veil, and an elaborate plan is developed with other Soul/Spirits who will not only play out their lives, but also interact with us. This is a plan only, a potential for how life events will happen, but at any time in that lifetime we have free will to change it as we go. This may be the lifetime in which you planned to take your Soul/Spirit to the next level by walking through the door to live a more expansive life in the Spirit while still on planet Earth.

What most "born again" or "spiritually awakened" individuals find challenging is the issue of karma, which is simply the stories of how individuals create relationships, and the ties that bind them together. Walking through the door into the spiritual life puts one major demand on us—there is no place for karmic experiences that were developed when we were in an imbalanced state in our previous lives. In the new spiritual life, there's no need for karmic experiences, as the relationships we develop in the new life are from a balance of mind and heart; respect and love for all develops, which makes us appear almost angelic to those around us.

Releasing old karmic ties brings us back to those cords that exist between ourselves and others. These ties must be severed if we hope to move completely into the spiritual life. To cut those ties, you need to say a prayer to God to help you release your old karmic ties so you can move ahead with your new life. Be sure to give thanks for His/Her assistance. After your prayer, sit in meditation, clearing your mind. Begin to visualize a cord attached to you and going out to another person. Visualize taking a pair of scissors and cutting the cord. Watch the cord return to the person. As you visualize the cord returning, say to yourself and to the other, "I release you from all karmic ties to me, and I send you my love." Now visualize all the people you've had a relationship with in this lifetime and visualize cords going out to each of them from you. Do the same as you did with the one person, and once again state, "I release you from all karmic ties, and I send you my love." Releasing old karmic ties doesn't mean you're cutting these people out of your life in the future. It simply means that the old life games you played with these people have come to an end, and the relationships developed in the future will be balanced, coming from both the heart and the mind with no judgment on your part toward them—only love for a fellow spiritual brother/sister.

Chapter 1

In the Beginning

*I*n the beginning was the Word, and the Word was with God, and the Word was God. The same was in the beginning with God. All things were made by him; and without him was not anything made that was made. In him was life; and the life was the light of men. And the light shineth in darkness; and the darkness comprehended it not. (John 1:1–5, KJV)

What an incredible biblical verse! I have marveled at and contemplated it many times over my lifetime. When one enters the spiritual life, the messages of the Bible become much clearer. We are told in the Christian church that God, the Creator, has existed for all time. He has no beginning and no end. He is omnipotent, knows all, and sees all.

God, the Creator of all, is energy. In the beginning, He was like the Adam of Genesis. His being was masculine in nature, and I hasten to add that it's not in the male perspective. He was a Creator of the mind. Just as John says, words are thoughts that come out of the mind of God. The Bible says that God created the earth as we know it in six days, and on the seventh day He rested; however, in the world of the Spirit, there is no such thing as time. Time is something we on earth use to make sense of our three-dimensional world. We live our life by the clock and calendars from the date of our birth until the day we die. Time is how we gauge our successes and failures in life, but God doesn't view us from this vantage point. He just sees us as spirits seeking to find our way back to Him as we play out our parts in this grand drama called life on earth.

From a theoretical point of view, God, like Adam, saw Himself as incomplete. In Genesis, Adam created the woman, Eve, from his rib to give him a companion. In the beginning, God also was incomplete and needed a balance. The Mother God became His balance. She brought the heart, and from the heart comes love. When we think of a mother, we think of a loving person who brought us into the world. God is seen as being wrathful and vengeful in the Old Testament. This is the mind of God at work. But we also see God in the New Testament as a loving and kind being. Throughout my life as a Christian, I've had a hard time trying to reconcile God as being both vengeful and kind.

According to Genesis, God created us in His image, and we too have a mind to control most of our existence in daily life. We also have a heart, which appears at times when we fall in love with another and when we create close relationships with others. But like our Father, we can be vengeful at times when we use our minds to rule over our daily lives.

For thousands of years on this planet, the minds of people, or the masculine, have ruled this world as they fight for survival or try to gain as much of what the world has to offer materially as they can. For eons of time, patriarchal societies have been the norm. Now and again, a matriarchal society, based on heart decisions, arose, but these have been few and far between. What's been missing throughout all of recorded history is a balanced society, governed by the head (the masculine) and the heart (the feminine). God, in His wisdom, created us as balanced spirits and souls, but very few have maintained that balance. Jesus, the Christ, and several of the great masters of previous times, have visited to remind us through their teachings and works that God's desire for everyone is to find the balance so that they can return to Him/Her.

Jesus extends to us a spiritual invitation: "Behold I stand at the door and knock, and whoever opens the door I will come in ..." The invitation from Jesus is to walk through that door to spirituality and become a balanced person who is ruled not only by the mind, but also by the heart of Mother/Father God.

Who Is Jesus?

Who is this person, Jesus? We know He was a mortal man who lived and taught about God's Kingdom two thousand years ago. We know He performed miracles and died at the hands of the Romans. We also know He rose from the dead after three days and ascended into heaven. The Christian faith since then has proclaimed him as our Savior and King. But who is Jesus Christ the King? I don't think we can answer that question until we go back to the beginning of time—to the creation of the world as it is written in the first book of the Bible.

Genesis 1:26 tells us that God created mankind in His image. This is one verse in the Bible that stirs up controversy. Biblical scholars for centuries have tried to make sense of what it means to be made "in God's image." What seems to get lost is who God is. What comes to mind for many Christians is the image of an old man with white, flowing hair, sitting on a throne in heaven and passing out judgments on humans after their lifetime on earth. What image do you have of God? What gets lost is the true nature of God. God is a spirit, and the only way we can be made in His image is if He gives a piece of His spirit to each of us at birth—hence, our soul, which is with us throughout our lifetime. It's a piece of God's spirit, and it returns to Him when we pass on.

Genesis 1 also tells us that God created the animals, birds, and sea life before He created humankind. We can probably hear the angels in heaven telling God to stop and not put humans on the planet, giving them free choice to make whatever decisions they'd like. That would be a recipe for disaster! But humans were the main part of God's plan for the earth. God wanted humans to be the rulers, or as some Bible translations say, have dominion over the entire earth and be the stewards over everything that grew or lived.

God's plan was for humans to be pure spirits and for their souls to be in direct connection with Him at all times. We know the story of the fall of humans in Genesis 3. We can accept the story as it is written and play the blame game on snakes and the woman, but I think the story is actually a metaphor of the free choice to follow God's will in our lives or to choose to wander off on our own path. Most humans don't connect with God for guidance, but instead venture out on their own solitary road map through life. Some, like the prodigal son, reconnect with God and follow Him to the end of their lives. Sadly, God had so much more for us to do on this earth than what we have done up to this point.

Remember, God asked us to rule over everything that grew and everything that was alive. Unfortunately, we've failed to be good stewards, and we've used the earth as our dumping ground. We've also interfered with the wildlife by killing or destroying it. By taking the route of selfishness, we've severed our ties with the earth and everything in it. God's intent was for us to honor the earth and everything in it. Think of how the indigenous of the world related to their surroundings. They were connected to the earth and creation, and everything was connected to them through

God. Over the centuries, we've become disconnected from God's creation. God sent Jesus Christ to bring back the balance between people, animal life, plant life, sea life, and the earth itself. I'd like to share with you how Jesus Christ as king can bring us back into harmony with each other and God's creation.

Jesus Christ became the new Adam for us to emulate. What made Him different from the rest of us? Like Adam, Jesus was a pure spirit. From the time He was a small child, He had a pure connection with God. He heard God speak to Him. Like us, He was given free choice in the decisions he had to make in His life, but the spiritual connection He had with God gave Him the ability to make decisions with a wisdom that came directly from the Lord. Wisdom is the gift God has given to many people throughout history: Moses, Joseph, Elijah, Elisha, Queen Esther, King David, King Solomon, and many others down to our present day. Only through a connection to God can we have that same wisdom from God in our lives. So where did the idea of Jesus Christ as king come from? The prediction of Jesus' birth came out of Old Testament scriptures in Isaiah and Micah, who spoke of the arrival of a king who would rule over Israel. In Matthew 2, wise men from the east searched for a baby who would become a king.

Throughout His entire life, Jesus was looked upon not only as a holy man speaking wisdom to the people, but also as the future King of Israel. During Jesus' lifetime, Rome occupied the Holy Land, and the regime was extremely oppressive and dictatorial. Every person wanted a king who would liberate and free them from this tyranny, and Jesus was the person they believed was sent from God, just as King David had been many years before.

In the scripture from John 18, we are confronted with Jesus as king when He is questioned by Pilate. Jesus didn't come out directly and say, "Yes, I am a king." Instead, He turned the question back on Pilate by saying that Pilate was the one calling him king. Jesus then made a profound statement: His kingdom was not of this world. Jesus was prophesying what His true mission was in this world. He was telling Pilate and the world that His kingdom would be a spiritual kingdom that would spread out across the world for thousands of years.

In His words, He was saying to everyone, "Follow Me. You too can be a king." For centuries, people who have sought to have that same relationship with God ask how it can be achieved. When we read passages from both the Old and New Testaments, we find examples of people who had the same spiritual connection as Jesus had with God. Think about Noah, who was told by God to build an ark to save him and his family when the flood came. Think of Moses, who developed a connection with God to perform the miracles to free the Israelites from Pharaoh. Think of his connection to God when he went up into the mountain to get the Ten Commandments. When Moses came down the mountain, his face glowed so brightly that he had to cover it when he met with others. Think of Elijah, who had such a strong spiritual connection with God that he was able to multiply the grain and oil for the widow and her son so that they would never starve. Think of the Apostle Peter in Acts 5:16 when he healed people just by them passing under his shadow.

In Mark 16, when Jesus met with His disciples after His resurrection, He commanded them to spread the good news that everyone could be connected to God and live under the Lord's direction for their lives. He went on to make some rather remarkable statements, indicating that God could protect them from injury or death if they drank something poisonous or got bitten by a deadly snake. These are miracles in themselves. Jesus also stated, "… they will place their hands on sick people, and they will get well" (Mark 16:18). He wasn't just saying this to His disciples, but also directly to you. In our prayers, we ask God to heal people we know, and we expect God to answer our prayers for others. Have you ever done what Jesus told us to do and lay hands on a sick person and healed them? Miracles take place when we have that spiritual connection to God.

I'd like to share my own experience of laying hands on a person, praying for healing, and seeing it happen. A few years ago, we had a Spirit-filled lady in her mid-eighties living near us as a neighbor. She'd suffered with an oozing ulcer on the ankle for ten years. She asked me to pray that the ulcer would be healed, so I put my hands on her bandaged ankle and prayed for her leg to be healed. Within three days, her leg healed and the ulcer never returned. That's what Jesus commanded His disciples to do, and that's what we can do if we develop the connection that Jesus, as well as many people over the centuries, had with God. To live the life God has for us, we too must open the door to God's Spirit connecting with our Spirit/Soul so that we can also be kings, just as Jesus Christ is King over all our lives.

Chapter 8
The Power of God

The word "power" is used eighty-three times in the Bible to refer to some aspect of God. We initially see the power of God in Genesis when He creates the earth out of seemingly nothing. Scientists refer to creation as the Big Bang, but they're also discovering that creation is in the quantum energy they are now seeing in a limited fashion using specialized microscopic equipment. They're discovering that the space that exists between everything that we can see with our eyes is really filled with quantum light energy particles and waves. In reality, all space and everything we can see is filled with the tiny, minute quantum particles that can be in more than one place at a time and can also travel through space, and even people, faster than the speed of light (186,000 miles per second). In fact, quantum light can instantaneously reach its destination.

Does it not seem strange that particles and waves of light that are so tiny even exist? Remember, it's only in the last hundred years that we've been able to see and measure radio and electrical waves, or even X-rays. The new frontier for research is this tiny particle of light that is an information carrier and a power source, just like the waves of light we now can see through our computerized technology. Does this not sound like science may have finally discovered how God created the universe? I am proposing the theory that quantum light particles and waves are God's Creative Energy. If this is the case, God is the Great Physicist who created the entire universe, including our own planet, from this special quantum energy. I'll leave it to scientists to verify the quantum energy theory once they're able to develop microscopes so powerful that they can either prove or refute my theory. If that becomes a reality, think of the advances in healthcare for all people. We could live hundreds of years, as many of the Old Testament patriarchs did. Maybe living five hundred years may not be appealing to many people, as eighty years is already really tough.

In this chapter, I'd like to show God's power in both the Old and New Testament, and then show you God's power today through personal anecdotes. King Jehoshaphat made this statement:

> Lord, the God of our ancestors, are you not the God who is in heaven? You rule over all the kingdoms of the nations. Power and might are

in your hand, and no one can withstand you. (2 Chronicles 20:6)

In this statement, God is equivalent to a human with hands. David also uses this analogy in Psalm 20:6: "Now this I know: The Lord gives victory to his anointed. He answers him from his heavenly sanctuary with the victorious power of his right hand." Isaiah recalls the power of God when He brought the people of Israel out of the land of Egypt:

Then his people recalled the days of old, the days of Moses and his people—where is he who brought them through the sea, with the shepherd of his flock? Where is he who sat his Holy Spirit among them, who sent his glorious arm of power to be at Moses's right-hand, who divided the waters before them, to gain for himself everlasting renown, who led them through the depths? (Isaiah 63:11)

Over the centuries, we've tried to make God appear to be like humans, only with massive power. We often refer to that power as coming from His arm or hand. Probably one of the most famous examples of the power of God is found in Exodus 19:20, when He descends on Mount Sinai just before giving Moses the Ten Commandments. In this passage, we don't see God in human form, but in majesty as a Spirit descending to meet with them.

> On the morning of the third day there was thunder and lightning, with a thick cloud over the mountain, and a very loud trumpet blast. Everyone in the camp trembled. Then Moses led the people out of the camp to meet with God, and they stood at the foot of the mountain. Mount Sinai was covered with smoke, because the Lord descended on it in fire. The smoke billowed out from it like smoke from a furnace, and the whole mountain trembled violently. As the sound of the trumpet grew louder and louder, Moses spoke and the voice of God answered him. (Exodus 19:16–19)

When God descends on Mount Sinai, we don't see a super-human with power flashing from His arm or hand. We see the mysterious energy from God showing Himself as awesome power that is unequalled anywhere. Humans are doubters at heart. We want to see proof of everything, including God, before we believe anything. How can you believe something you cannot see? People don't accept Christian beliefs unless they see some kind of proof. In our twenty-first century belief system, we reject anything that's not scientifically proven. We've become so inundated with information from social media that our beliefs get shaped by those who believe as we do. Faith cannot be based on information we hear or see, but we look for proof of faith that cannot be found. We have failed to see God, who is alive and well and working through people every day.

In the New Testament, Jesus shows us how God's power can work through people. We're aware of the healings Jesus did during His ministry, but Jesus also used the power of God to deal with the weather.

> One day Jesus said to his disciples, "Let us go over to the other side of the lake." So they got into a boat and set out. As they sailed, he fell asleep. A squall came down on the lake, so that the boat was being swamped, and they were in great danger. The disciples went and woke him, saying, "Master, Master, we're going to drown!" He got up and rebuked the wind and the raging waters, the storm subsided, and all was calm. "Where is your faith?" He asked his disciples. (Luke 8:22–24).

God can give that same power to people like you and me, if we have that total connection with Him through our Spirit/Soul. I know this, because I have personally witnessed it in my own life.

A few years ago, I was living in Orillia, Ontario, Canada when an EF-1 tornado came through our area and toppled a huge tree branch onto the roof of our house, causing severe damage to the shingles. Many people who've been through tornadoes report that they sound like a train coming through their yard. That was the sound we heard, so I rushed the entire family to the basement. I was just starting down the stairs myself when I said to my family, "You might as well forget it. It's already gone by." When you've gone through a tornado, you learn how fast they can come and go.

Approximately two weeks later, my daughter and I were standing outside our house on the front step when suddenly we saw the funnel of another tornado coming directly at us. This time we didn't run when we saw it. I don't know what came over me, but I closed my eyes and stretched out my arm toward the tornado and said without thinking, "In the name of Jesus Christ, I command you to be gone!" In my mind's eye, I saw a lightning bolt go out from my hand to the tornado, and I saw the tornado and the clouds begin to roll backward from the direction they came. I opened my eyes and saw the same thing happening. The only way to describe it was like watching a video running in reverse. Neither my daughter nor I could believe what had just happened. We saw the power of God that day working through a human who is connected to God through his Spirit/Soul.

Throughout my life, I've been through five tornados, and to this day I get a little anxious when a storm comes and

I know a tornado will develop out of it. I'd like to share a second experience I had when I was in the middle of an EF-4 tornado thirty years ago. If you google the Barrie, Ontario, Canada tornado of 1985, you'll find write-ups that will show you the power of this highly destructive storm that caused death and massive destruction in a city. This storm hit in the middle of my wife's battle with cancer. I was driving alone, heading north on the major multi-lane highway from the hospital in Toronto to my home in Orillia. Halfway home, the sky turned black in the middle of the afternoon; even the headlights couldn't pierce the darkness. Everyone began pulling off to the side of the highway as the wind began to intensify. As I sat in my car, I began to pray, using the same prayers I used in the previous tornado. The car began to rock violently but stayed on all four wheels. Within five minutes, the storm passed and the sun came out. The damage all around me was devastating. A quarter of a mile down the road I saw a complete farmer's shed sitting in the median.

What did I learn from that experience? For one thing, I was sending out my prayers in the middle of the storm. Secondly, God's power doesn't just move destructive weather away from us for our protection. Often God's hand saves us in the middle of a storm. When you see the aftermath of tornadoes and hurricanes, you wonder how anyone survived The answer is God is alive and well and answers prayers all the time. Our problem is that we have difficulty understanding the mystery of God.

Chapter 9
Cleansing of the Holy Spirit

Throughout His ministry, Jesus taught His followers about life in His Kingdom by using parables. Some of the parables contained references to farming and growing seeds. There's nothing more important to a farmer than a huge yield of grain. The more grain to sell or use, the more money he gets to live on for the next year. I think we can understand why Jesus talked about grain crops to illustrate the richness of the Kingdom of Heaven, especially when we are the grain in His crop.

I'd like to share with you a farming story out of my youth. I grew up on a farm in Southern Ontario. Things haven't really changed much since that time, except for the machinery and the number of acres you have to farm now to make a living. Today, farmers have combines to bring in the grain. I'll always remember grain harvesting time. When the grain was ripe, my dad would cut it using a binder, which cut and wrapped several of the stalks together into what we called a sheaf. One of the neighbors owned a threshing machine. All the farmers would come together to help each other thresh the grain. It was always a special occasion, as the women would also come together to cook meals that would just blow your mind. This was a Christian community in action. The men brought the sheaves of grain in from the fields to the threshing machine. With lots of pulleys, conveyer belts, and sickle-like knives, the grain separated from the straw, and the chopped-up straw and chaff would be blown out the back pipe to collect on the ground. My father's job was to climb up on the mound of straw, level it, and build it into a huge mound. When my father came off that mound, you could hardly recognize him. He'd be totally black from the dirt that stuck to his sweating body.

Now let's step back from that vision you have of a man totally covered in dirt. Jesus used the parables of the seeds to illustrate God's Word, and I think of the grain that separated out in the threshing machine as the treasures that the farmers sought when they harvested the crops. What about the chaff and straw that piled up in that huge mound? Using Jesus' analogy, the straw serves little purpose except as bedding for animals, but if the grain is God's Word for us, we can look at the straw and chaff as the impediments to our growth as Christians and followers of God. I'd like to metaphorically compare that pile of straw to the sins that enter us through-out our lifetimes. Our sins build up, and we never seem to be rid of them. The Apostle Paul decried this when he said in Romans 7:14–20:

> We know that the law is spiritual; but I am unspiritual, sold as a slave to sin. I do not understand what I do. For what I want to do I do not do, but what I hate I do. And if I do what I do not want to do, I agree that the law is good. As it is, it is no longer I myself who do it, but it is sin living in me. For I know that good itself does not dwell in me, that is, in my sinful nature. For I have the desire to do what is good, but I cannot carry it out. For I do not do the good I want to do, but the evil I do not want to do—this I keep on doing. Now if I do what I do not want to do, it is no longer I who do it, but it is sin living in me that does it.

We find ourselves in the same struggle today. So what is the solution to this challenge we all face? I'd like to share the response Jesus has for us as it is written in Matthew 3:13–17:

> Then Jesus came from Galilee to the Jordan to be baptized by John. But John tried to deter him saying, "I need to be baptized by you, and you come to me?" Jesus replied, "Let it be so now; it is proper for us to do this to fulfill all

righteousness." Then John consented. As soon as Jesus was baptized, he went up out of the water. At that moment heaven was opened, and he saw the Spirit of God descending like a dove and lighting on him. And a voice from heaven said, "This is my son, whom I love; with him I am well pleased."

Did Jesus really need to be baptized? Jesus was without sin, unlike Paul and us, who rail against sin. In His baptism, Jesus provides the example for Christians to follow. He points out the importance of ridding ourselves of all sin, with the water washing all sins away. The descent of the Holy Spirit was God's way of showing us that once we release the sin from our lives, the Dove from Heaven, or the Holy Spirit, can fill us so we can have a relationship with Him.

The sins that come to mind are easy to deal with. We can pray for forgiveness and seek forgiveness from those we have sinned against. But what about the sins that have accumulated over a lifetime that we don't remember anymore? They could be mistakes against others or against ourselves. What about the angry moments against others that still reside as sin in our emotions? Or what about the discrimination against someone or a group different from us that still resides as sin in our belief systems? Your beliefs may be totally different today because Jesus Christ is in your life, but like Paul experienced, the old sins are still there.

I'd like to share with you an example of the sins that build up in people's lives. When I was growing up, my late aunt and her next-door farm neighbor had an issue arise between them. They both attended the local church, and for forty years neither one of them spoke to the other. Whatever happened, the pain of that event was so deep they couldn't get past it or deal with it. When both were late in life, one of them broke the silence and asked the other if she remembered what the problem was that drove them apart. Incredibly, neither one of those ladies could remember the issue.

At the time of the Reformation, Martin Luther still believed that confession, which was part of the original church, should be practiced—but not necessarily with a priest or penitence. He identified three practices he believed were needed to rid ourselves of all sins: (1) Daily confession to God in prayer. Are we faithful in our prayers each day to seek God's forgiveness? (2) Public confession in the common liturgical confession of sins. Rather than saying nothing, we immediately need to seek forgiveness of another for a wrong done in public. (3) Personal confession before a fellow Christian, including a confession of concrete sins and a personally addressed absolution. This is often tough to do, but talking honestly to a family member or friend about a wrong-doing stops it from being buried in ourselves for years.

As you know, confession has moved far down on our priority list. It's less emphasized today; instead, we go to see a psychologist or psychiatrist when we have problems. Instead of clearing out our sins, the helping professions stir them up. Jesus Christ is the answer to our problems with sin.

> "He himself bore our sins" in his body on the cross, so that we might die to sins and live for righteousness; "by his wounds you have been healed." For "you were like sheep going astray," but now you have returned to the Shepherd and Overseer of your souls. (1 Peter 2:24–25)

I'd like you to do something to illustrate what it means to have built-up sins in our bodies that have not been cleared, preventing us from living a full and fulfilling life in Christ. Fill a glass half full with some stones. The stones represent the sins we haven't dealt with in our lives as Christians. Now fill the glass with water. The glass looks full, but is it? Empty the water out of the glass and into an empty glass of the same size. As you can see, the glass is only partially full. Think of the water as the Holy Spirit trying to send His Light into you, but the sins of the past only allow a small amount of the Spirit to enter and reside within you. With the stones removed, God can fully enter your life and create the relationship and communion He wishes to have with you. The challenge I put out to you today is to examine yourself to see if you have anything in your life that may be buried and forgotten that is stopping the Holy Spirit from totally filling you. If so, I encourage you to take it to the Lord in prayer.

Chapter 10

Our Work Begins with the Lord

Matthew 4 sets the stage for Jesus' experience during His forty days in the desert by describing His baptism by John the Baptist in the Jordan River, and the Spirit of God descending on Him. Why would Jesus need forty days in the desert alone with God? Was it to expose him to Satan's temptations, as seems to be indicated in Matthew 4:1? I believe there's more to it than just being tempted and giving Jesus the chance to rebuke His nemesis.

Forty is a very common number in the Bible, and each time it appears it seems to have significance in the lives of the people. Genesis 7:4 tells us that the Noah flood lasted for forty days and forty nights. The result of that flood was renewal of all the earth. Mankind was starting over again. Then you have the Exodus of the Israelites from Egypt, which lasted for forty years. Once again it proved to be a renewal for the people of Israel, who started again in the Promised Land. During their wandering in the desert, Moses went up in the mountain for forty days to get the Ten Commandments from the Lord. Once again, the laws laid out a new beginning for the Israelites. King David reigned over Israel for forty years, as did Solomon during a time of greatness in leadership for the people. As well, there were forty days between Jesus' resurrection and Pentecost.

I believe that the forty days Jesus spent in the desert prepared Him for His work in ministry and healing. Can we wrap our heads around forty days without food? Most of us can't go without eating for a single day. Jesus needed this period of time with God; this was His preparation time to spiritually learn what He needed in order to preach and heal. We too need preparation for doing a job—often it's called school, college, university, or on the job training. No one can jump into a job without preparation. To be spiritually connected to God, we too need special preparatory time, which includes Bible reading, daily meditation and prayer, and our time in church worshiping and praising God.

I'd like to take a minute and tell you of my spiritual preparation that began thirty-five years ago. At that time, our family was going through a crisis, and I felt I was a total failure. In tears, I fell to my knees and prayed to God, saying that I had totally failed my family and Him. At that moment, I asked the Lord to forgive me and take over and guide me from then on. I did what Jesus asked us to do in Revelations 3:20–22, when He said:

I stand at the door and knock. If anyone hears my voice and opens the door, I will come in and eat with that person, and they with me. To the one who is victorious, I will give the right to sit with me on my throne, just as I was victorious and sat down with my Father on his throne. Whoever has ears, let him hear what the Spirit says to the churches.

Shortly after that experience, God put me through what I can only describe as a Damascus Road experience, similar to what the Apostle Paul went through but without the blindness. I saw visions of our Lord, and I can only describe this new beginning as going back to school, only it was Spiritual School. I began to crave books on Christianity, spiritualism, and how to serve God. I'm not up to forty years yet in my preparation, but I can honestly say that the Bible became my favorite book. As of the last count, I've read it thirty-two times cover to cover. Over the years, I've been tempted as Jesus was, but so far I have resisted the dark side's attempts to control me. We see what happened to Jesus when Satan saw Him in a weakened state, just as what happens to us in moments when we become tired and weak. I believe that, like Jesus, I needed to have my spiritual work, which has lasted for thirty-five years. I am slowly getting there. Maybe forty is my number as well.

I'd like to look at Satan's attempts to control Jesus in Matthew 4:3–10. Jesus, after forty days without food, would have been extremely weak. Satan knew that Jesus had the power from God to turn rocks into bread. Remember, God rained down manna from heaven in the dew to feed the Israelites when they were in the desert for forty years. Manna is a tiny seed that could be formed into bread. For six days each week they collected the manna. If Jesus was God's Son, He could receive manna from heaven, but God had bigger plans for Jesus. Think of the miracles Jesus performed during His ministry. Just after His experience in the desert, Jesus was at a wedding in Cana and was asked by His mother to turn water into high quality wine, which he did. Matthew 15:35–38 describes how Jesus fed a crowd of at least four thousand people with only seven loaves of bread and a few small fish:

> He told the crowd to sit down on the ground. Then he took the seven loaves and the fish, and when he had given thanks, he broke them and gave them to the disciples, and they in turn to the people. They all ate and were satisfied. Afterward the disciples picked up seven basketsful of broken pieces that were left over. The number of those who ate was four thousand men, besides women and children.

Jesus responded to the devil in the desert by saying, "One does not live by bread alone, but by every word that comes from the mouth of God." As a pastor once said, we as Christians straddle two worlds, with one foot in the present materialistic world, and one foot in the spiritual world of God. Where are our priorities for living?

As you can see, Satan never stops with just one temptation ... you can be guaranteed another will come. He looks for our weaknesses and then tries to take advantage of us, just as he tried with Jesus. In the second temptation, Satan took Jesus to the pinnacle of the temple in Jerusalem and basically said, "Jump." He told Jesus that the angels would not let any injury happen to him. Satan knew that God would protect Him, but if Jesus jumped, it would be Satan who would win by forcing Jesus to do something He didn't want to do, because it was challenging God's authority and power. Jesus knew the power of God to heal, and during His ministry, Jesus healed many people of every sickness, disease, and frailty going.

I know the power of God to heal, and I'll share my own story with you. When I was growing up, I was told by my church family that God, through His servants, healed people in biblical times, but that miracles don't happen now. In the 1960s, the "God is dead" movement began. The belief was that God created the universe, galaxies, and the planet Earth, and then set everything on auto pilot while He left to go back to heaven and watch over His creation. I had an experience that convinced me that God is totally active in His creation and is omnipresent in our world.

Three months after my late wife passed on from brain cancer, I took my thirteen year old daughter on a downhill skiing vacation to Jay Peak Mountain in Vermont. It snowed the first night, and freezing rain came down on the mountain. We were up early to ski, and the skiing was fast on the ice and slow when we hit patches of new snow. At one point, we cut across from one trail to another. I hit a patch of ice, but my skis weren't sharp enough to handle it. I skittered off the trail and fell about twenty feet into a ravine. My fall was stopped when I hit a tree across my chest. It was the worst, sickening thud I've ever experienced. Fortunately, my daughter was following me and summoned help. I remained conscious the whole time. The only way I can describe the injury was that my chest felt like it was ripped wide open.

At that moment, I said a prayer to God: "Lord, my body is badly broken. If you still have work for me to do on this earth, I need healing. If it's your will, I'm prepared to come home to you." Suddenly, I felt as if warm honey was being poured all over me. I was taken to the local Vermont hospital, where I was diagnosed with a bruised heart and broken sternum. The bruised heart sent my enzyme levels through the roof. Since the hospital didn't have a heart unit if surgery was needed, I was transferred to Montreal General by ambulance. All I can remember was being tested and X-rayed all night.

Over the next few days, I had visits from multiple doctors who were trying to figure out what had happened to me. By the time I reached Montreal General, the enzyme levels had returned to normal, indicating that the heart had returned to normal and the sternum didn't require surgery. The doctors were totally baffled by what they saw and couldn't believe what had happened. One week later, my daughter returned to me from the Vermont family who looked after her, and we drove back home to Ontario. That week, God proved to me that miracles are still part of our world. As we look around this world, we see miracles happening every day, such as spontaneous remissions from disease. God is alive and well in this world today, and I am living proof of that.

From the scripture reading, we see that the devil wasn't quite finished with Jesus. He took Him to a high mountain and offered Him all the kingdoms of the world; all He had to do was fall down and worship Satan. At that time, Rome ruled almost all of the known world. Satan knew that the people who would follow Jesus would believe He was the savior who would re-establish King David's throne and rid Israel of the Roman Empire. Once again, Jesus rejected Satan, saying, "Away from me, Satan! For it is written: 'Worship the Lord your God, and serve him only.'" Jesus knew that He would not create a throne for Himself in Israel at that time. His kingdom would not be a physical kingdom, but a spiritual one that would not just last a few years, but thousands of years. We are part of Christ's spiritual kingdom, helping

Him spread the light of God through the work of the Holy Spirit to all the world. That is our mission for this life. How are we doing? Sometimes it looks like we're taking one step forward and two back, but if we accept God's guidance in our lives, we'll take two steps forward and sometimes only one back. Peace on earth through God's Spirit is ahead of us if we don't falter. Let's open our hearts and minds to Psalm 119:18, a prayer for spiritual insight. We ask God: "Open thou mine eyes, that I may behold wondrous things out of thy law" (KJV).

Chapter 11
God Is Love

The nature of God has been debated for centuries. The Old Testament strongly indicates that judgment based on the Covenant Law He gave to the people of Israel was His true nature—a vindictive God who would harshly judge His people if they failed to follow them. Suddenly, at Jesus' birth, we see God make a 180 degree turn in His nature and promote peace and reconciliation among individuals and all the people of the earth. How could God have two natures?

Thirty-four years ago, when I awakened spiritually to the reality of God and Jesus Christ, his Son, I was given a glimpse into His true nature. When I walked through the door to accept God's Spirit into my life, I underwent what is described in Acts 9 as the Damascus Road experience of Saul, who became the Apostle Paul. The Lord showed me visions and directions for my life. In one vision, I was taken into heaven in spirit to have a brief view and experience of the afterlife. Some people who've had a near death experience report a similar experience. I saw animals that are enemies on earth feeding together, just like the description of the new heaven and new earth in Isaiah 65:25: "The wolf and the lamb will feed together, and the lion will eat straw like the ox, and dust will be the serpent's food. They will neither harm nor destroy on all my holy mountain." In that vision I felt LOVE that was so wonderful I didn't want to return to my earthly body. I just wanted to stay and pet the lion, because the love I felt was so strong and nothing like the love we experience on the earthly plane. The experience of that incredible feeling will stay with me for all time, and I know that it awaits me when I pass over in death to rejoin that phenomenal experience once again.

Are there really two aspects of God—one part totally judgmental and vindictive and the other part pure love? I don't believe we have two gods in one. The Old Testament seems to be more judgmental, but if you look at God's actions, we see Him as being deeply concerned for His chosen people of Israel. First of all, when God created the universe, He did it out of love. Genesis 1:31 shows us His true nature: "God saw all that He had made, and it was very good." Man and woman had a choice to make in the Garden of Eden, and they chose to go their own way, not the way God intended them to take.

God gave humans the quality of free choice, and we continue to exercise that privilege. GOD IS PURE LOVE! As human parents, we may not like what our children say and do, but we stand aside and let them have free choice, even though we know some of their actions may hurt them physically, emotionally, mentally, and even spiritually. God gave that same free choice to all humans, and we in turn try to do the same for our children, even though we may counsel them against taking a particular action. Even though God is pure love, He/She is prepared to send warnings to us in various ways, but the final decision is ours and not God's.

When we make decisions that are evil in nature, we often blame it on the devil, or a fallen angel called Satan. Let's examine that evil philosophy for a moment. If God is a Spirit and is in the quantum particles of light, then what is Satan? Logically speaking, our view of a being that is like a raging beast with horns doesn't make much sense, but we like to humanize spiritual beings, such as God and Satan. If we look at Satan in the same light as God, he is also quantum energy. If the energy of God is love and pure light, then we have to assume Satan's energy is the opposite and is dark energy. Remember that everything in physics has polar opposites. In magnetism, there is a north pole and a south pole; things are up or down, in or out, black or white. These last two lead us to the nature of God and Satan.

First of all, God represents everything that is pure, creative, and filled with light. The dark energy of Satan represents the polar opposite, which can be compared to humanity's use of free choice to make their own ego-driven decisions. With the use of free choice over millennia, the dark energy of Satan, or the polar opposite of God, has become the ruling energy of the world. That dark energy has led to people to only consider themselves when they make decisions. Division among nations has led to wars and hatreds that have lasted for centuries. Where is God in all of this? Many people have metaphorically dragged God onto their side in a war. Some wars see God participating on both sides of a conflict. Much as we'd like to have God on our side, answering our prayers for success, God is not there. If God is pure love and light, it's impossible for Him/Her to go where there is no light. If God entered a dark room, it would be like turning on a light switch. We all know what happens when a light is turned on—darkness flees. You could live your whole life living in the darkness of free choice, but if you walk through Christ's door and let God into your life, the darkness has to flee. If you're truly intent on following God, the light will expose the areas in your life that need to be dealt with and moved out to make room for the infilling of God's balanced light.

For thousands of years, God has stood by and let humans do their thing as they use their skills and power to get what they want out of life. For that entire time, God has tried to counteract the dark energies that have enveloped earth. In the Old Testament, He found individuals who let His light in, and they became His spokesmen to try to change peoples' attitudes and ways and turn them back to God, who would guide them in the light. Prophet after prophet spoke God's words. When you read what many of the prophets said, it sounds as if the message was coming from an angry, vengeful God, who would bring disaster down on them if they didn't return to the Covenant Law He gave them.

The Laws that God gave to the people of Israel have been termed The Ten Commandments. When you read these commands, the light of God shines through, and we see His attempt to influence humans to live in the pure love of God. Let's consider each of these commandments of love to the people of Israel and to us in the twenty-first century. Exodus 20:3–17 contains the Ten Commandments, but verse 20 gives Moses' interpretation of God's purpose for giving them to the people: "Do not be afraid. God has come to test you, so that the fear of God will be with you to keep you from sinning." That doesn't sound like a nice God, but one who will exact judgment on anyone who breaks the rules. Even Moses, who was close to God, didn't fully understand who God was.

The first commandment states: "You shall have no other gods before me" (v. 1). I believe that the negativity of how the commandments are given paint a picture of a vengeful God; however, putting anything else above the light of God will negate any chance the person will return to a pure connection with the Creator.

The second commandment states: "You shall not make for yourself an image in the form of anything in heaven above or on the earth beneath or in the waters below. You shall not bow down to them or worship them; for I, the Lord your God, am a jealous God, punishing the children for the sin of the parents to the third and fourth generation of those who hate me, but showing love to a thousand generations of those who love me and keep my commandments" (vv. 4–6). In this commandment, God challenges the very free choice that He gave the people. He sees the darkness that humans create when they make their own images and follow or bow down to them, and He knows it will result in disaster, not just for themselves, but for their children and grandchildren who will be led astray. Following their own dark path can only lead to disaster, and generations will miss God's light entirely.

The third commandment states: "You shall not misuse the name of the Lord your God, for the Lord will not hold anyone guiltless who misuses his name" (v. 7). As was stated previously in this chapter, wars have been fought in the name of God. This is just one example of using God's name to give credence to what a person does. When you try to mix God's light with darkness, the only result can be a revealing of the evil that previously lay hidden.

The fourth commandment tells us to take one day of the week to bring our minds and hearts back to God: "Remember the Sabbath day by keeping it holy. Six days you shall labor and do all your work, but the seventh day is a Sabbath to the Lord your God. On it you shall not do any work, neither you, nor your son or daughter, nor your male or female servant, nor your animals, nor any foreigner residing in your towns.

For in six days the Lord made the heavens and the earth, the sea, and all that is in them, but he rested on the seventh day. Therefore the Lord blessed the Sabbath day and made it holy" (vv. 8–11). Once again, we see God reaching out to remind us to seek the Lord and His light. This commandment asks us to consider God in everything we do, and His love will be at the center of it.

The fifth commandment states: "Honor your father and your mother, so that you may live long in the land the Lord your God is giving you" (v. 12). Many cultures have adopted ancestor worship as part of their religious ceremonies. It's based on respect and love for those who were part of our family. When we look at it from God's perspective, all people on earth have a piece of God in them, and everyone, including our parents, deserve to be treated in the same way you would treat God.

The sixth through the tenth commandments talk about how we deal with other people: "You shall not murder. You shall not commit adultery. You shall not steal. You shall not give false testimony against your neighbor. You shall not covet your neighbor's house. You shall not covet your neighbor's wife, or his male or female servant, his ox or donkey, or anything that belongs to your neighbor" (vv. 13–17). Like the respect due your parents, God lays out a respect for everyone else, because going against these commandments means accepting the darkness and not the light and love of God.

Even though many of the commandments are written from a negative perspective, God appears to us as a father trying to teach His child not to do things that will hurt him or her. "Don't touch that hot stove or you'll get burnt." God worries about our safety and doesn't want to see us hurt by actions that honor the dark side of our nature. Consequences are a part of every action we take. In physics, this is called, "for every action there is an equal and opposite reaction." In spiritual terms, every action taken in the dark side results in an equal and opposite action that builds up in our emotional, mental, spiritual, or physical body. The same is true when our actions or words align with God's plan for us; the balanced light and love of God will also build up equally in our four bodies. God makes the promise that when we honor our mother and father, "we may live long in the land the Lord your God is giving you." Some of us are discovering that we are able, through His Spirit, to live longer lives.

The Bible is a remarkable book and really should be called a Book of Love. Would you believe that the word "love" is used 334 times in the Old Testament and 280 times in the New Testament? An entire book in the Old Testament is devoted to love: the Song of Songs, or Song of Solomon, as some translations call it. When you read it, a romance novel comes to mind. The number of times love is spoken of in the Bible certainly shows the Creator of all to be the GOD OF LOVE. Probably no chapter in the Old Testament sums up this aspect of His/Her character as well as Psalm 136:

- Give thanks to the Lord, for he is good. His love endures forever.
- Give thanks to the God of gods. His love endures forever.
- Give thanks to the Lord of lords; His love endures forever.
- To him who alone does great wonders. His love endures forever.
- Who by his understanding made the heavens. His love endures forever.
- Who spread out the earth upon the waters. His love endures forever.
- Who made the great lights. His love endures forever.
- The sun to govern the day. His love endures forever.
- The moon and stars to govern the night. His love endures forever.
- To him who struck down the firstborn of Egypt. His love endures forever.
- And brought Israel out from among them. His love endures forever.
- With a mighty hand and outstretched arm. His love endures forever.
- To him who divided the Red Sea asunder. His love endures forever.

- And brought Israel through the midst of it. His love endures forever.
- But swept Pharaoh and his army into the Red Sea. His love endures forever.
- To him who led his people through the wilderness. His love endures forever.
- To him who struck down great kings. His love endures forever.
- And that killed the mighty kings. His love endures forever.
- Sihon king of the Amorites. His love endures forever.
- And Og king of Bashan. His love endures forever.
- And gave their land as an inheritance. His love endures forever.
- An inheritance to his servant Israel. His love endures forever.
- He remembered us in our low estate. His love endures forever.
- And freed us from our enemies. His love endures forever.
- He gives food to every creature. His love endures forever.
- Give thanks to the God of heaven. His love endures forever.

Throughout the Old Testament, we see the people of Israel, who have been given a special status as the people God, choose to work through and show the world how they too could live according to His precepts and become people of God. The people in the nations surrounding Israel were considered to be living in darkness, also in need of the light and love God was offering. Ironically, even the people of Israel couldn't stay in God's light; they too wandered into the darkness, so God sent prophet after prophet to get them to return to His light and love, but to no avail. I don't believe the God of light and love exacted revenge and judgment on the people of Israel, but He could no longer protect them with that light. In the end, they were conquered time and again and either sent into slavery in another country or forced to live under the brutal tyranny of the Romans.

Many believe God changed in the New Testament and became the God of love when He sent Jesus to earth to proclaim a new way of living in His Light. Probably the most famous verse in the New Testament is John 3:16: "For God so loved the world that he gave his one and only Son, that whoever believes in him shall not perish but have eternal life." What gets lost in this famous verse is that each of us, when we connect our Spirit/Soul to Him, can become sons and daughters of God. The promise of eternal life is a return to reconnect our Spirit/Soul with the Creator God, who is pure love.

Jesus gave a message to those who followed Him, and it continues to be the message God wants all people to hear and act on. It's been called the Sermon on the Mount, and also the Beatitudes, and it's found in Matthew 5:3–11. Each verse begins with "Blessed," which means a holy message from God. If God is love, then each verse has an even more profound meaning for us if "Loved" replaces "Blessed."

- Loved are the poor in spirit, for theirs is the kingdom of heaven.
- Loved are those who mourn, for they will be comforted.
- Loved are the meek, for they will inherit the earth.
- Loved are those who hunger and thirst for righteousness, for they will be filled.
- Loved are the merciful, for they will be shown mercy.
- Loved are the pure in heart, for they will see God.
- Loved are the peacemakers, for they will be called children of God.
- Loved are those who are persecuted because of righteousness, for theirs is the kingdom of heaven.
- Loved are you when people insult you, persecute you and falsely say all kinds of evil against you because of me.

From personal experience, I can honestly say that when you make the connection between your Spirit/Soul and the Creator God, you can never go back to living life in darkness.

Living in the light is far superior to living life controlled by your own ego and the power of other people's desires to influence you. Peace of mind comes over you, and fear can no longer envelope your life.

From my experience teaching social psychology at the university level, I believe most people live in fear of something. Sometimes it's as simple as the fear of what people might say about them. This has become an epidemic on social media, where anyone can write anything with anonymity, depriving the offended party of the opportunity to confront the person in person. Sadly, our Internet freedom has two sides to it. It's great for sharing information, but it carries a dark side to it in that anyone can say anything without repercussion. The rise of fake news and other deception is the darkness taking over something that was created to be an institution of God's light. Once again, we're challenged to rise above fear and move to the light and love of God for our direction in life. We have to remember that just because someone is spouting hate, it doesn't mean that they don't have the Spirit/ Soul of God in them. They just haven't turned on the light and love in their lives to receive the divine guidance of God. Remember what Jesus said in Matthew 5:44–48:

> But I tell you, love your enemies and pray for those who persecute you, that you may be children of your Father in heaven. He causes his sun to rise on the evil and the good, and sends rain

on the righteous and the unrighteous. If you love those who love you, what reward will you get? Are not even the tax collectors doing that? And if you greet only your own people, what are you doing more than others? Do not even pagans do that? Be perfect, therefore, as your Heavenly Father is perfect.

LOVE knows no bounds!

Chapter 12
God in Our Relationships

When we think of relationships, we usually think of friends, co-workers, spouses, and families; however, relationships begin long before we are even born. Our relationship begins with God. In Psalm 139:13, David speaks of God's hand in his birth: "For you created my inmost being; you knit me together in my mother's womb." Jeremiah 1:4–5 gives us a similar message from God: "The word of the Lord came to me, saying, 'Before I formed you in the womb I knew you, before you were born I set you apart; I appointed you as a prophet to the nations.'" Even within the womb, God is with us and seeks to guide our lives.

For eons of time, people have debated when life begins. What we fail to understand is that God is in relationship with everything and everyone, no matter what our age. God is the Great Physicist who works through the quantum light energy to create all things, including us. Is it really a surprise that God is also our Creator in the womb? What makes our relationship with God so unique is that there are no two individuals on earth that are the same. Our DNA is unique to only one person out of the 7.5 billion people on earth. Even your mother and father aren't exact duplicates of you, but they do bring together the special DNA that serves as the blueprint for the purpose of every cell in your body. Your genes become God's construction crew to put that unique body of yours together in the womb. God is the awesome Creator.

For a child's first six years, he/she is like a sponge, and massive learning takes place. Have you ever looked into a baby's eyes and seen pure wisdom? God is still very close to every baby in those first few years of life. He even controls the amount of energy a baby's brain gives off, as reported by neurologist Dr. Rima Laibow in the book *Quantitative EEG and Neurofeedback*. Up to six years of age, small children have brain waves in the .5 Hz. to 8 Hz. zone, which is very low compared to adults who have up to 35 Hz. The low brain waves give young children the ability to take in massive amounts of information as they learn to walk, speak, and gain an understanding of their environment. Maybe now we see why adults can't learn at the same pace as young children; however, there is a down side to the massive learning that takes place in childhood. The more knowledge a child takes in, the farther away from God he/she moves. As brain activity increases in the beta range, the less God's voice can come through to a person.

Let's consider the story of the boy Samuel in the Old Testament. He lived with Eli the priest to train to be a man of God in the temple; however, God had plans for Samuel's life. In the middle of the night, when Samuel's brain was functioning in the lower Hz, God called to him. At first, Samuel thought it was his master, Eli, calling him. Three times this happened, until finally Eli realized that it was God trying to speak directly to Samuel: "The Lord came and stood there, calling as at the other times, 'Samuel, Samuel!' Then Samuel said, 'Speak, for your servant is listening'" (1 Samuel 3:10). How many times has God called out to you, but you thought you were hearing things, or that someone else was calling to you?

Throughout our lives, God tries to reach us. Just remember … God will never force Himself/Herself upon you. You have your Spirit/Soul within you, which is a piece of God's Spirit that you received at birth. Like God, our earthly mothers and fathers love us unconditionally, but they would never interfere with our life choices. They might not agree with our choices, but they still love us unconditionally. Our parents, who lovingly raised us, serve as the pattern of how relationships should function. Our Lord sets the example of how perfect parents raise their children; they don't necessarily like everything children do, but they still love them unconditionally.

Every family has rules to live by in order to function in respectful relationships. God also gave His family rules to live by in the Ten Commandments, which are also based on love and respect for everyone else and their property. Interestingly, God set out ten very simple but profoundly powerful rules. But then what did we do as a society? We added more rules. Just look at the Old Testament book of Leviticus. Moses didn't seem to think God's Ten Commandments were enough, so he added regulations to flesh out details for living, acting, and even eating.

Humans love details and guidance in their lives. Governments at all levels create laws and regulations to control every aspect of our lives, so instead of creating a spiritual connection between our Spirit/Soul and God's Spirit, we rely on someone or something else to tell us what we can and cannot do. For example, God says in Exodus 20:13, 15: "You shall not murder … you shall not steal." If you are connected to God, the last thing you'd ever do is kill another person or steal from him/her. Since so many people aren't connected in this way, society creates a law with enough teeth in it to persuade people not to do it. If they break that law, they will be severely penalized. Obviously, our man-made laws don't seem to be doing the job. So what is the answer? Humankind has only one alternative—recognize that God is alive and well on this planet and help people see the bigger picture of the God of Creation and the God in us.

Our problem is that we don't see other people and the earth the way God sees them. Let's first look at how we see each other in our own culture. From a sociological perspective, humans need relationships with other humans. We cannot live solitary lives by excluding other people and living like hermits. We are beings who are constantly learning, and we need other people in our lives to help us with those learning experiences. Sociologists tell us that the people we attract are like mirrors in which we can see our true selves. These people can either compliment our belief systems and reinforce our thoughts, or challenge our values and beliefs, which may lead us to develop a totally different set of beliefs. The challenge is to deal with people who literally drive us nuts and remain in our lives no matter what we do. Obviously, we part ways with them when the life lesson is complete.

I have always looked on people who come into my life as gifts. Some gifts are with us for a short period of time, and some are with us for a lifetime. Regardless of the length of time they're with us, we are constantly learning and changing our values and belief systems. There is always something missing in our lives when we rely solely on other humans to be our influencers. As we discussed earlier, a child is as close to God as one can get. Jesus pointed this out in Matthew 18:2–5:

> He called a little child to him, and placed the
> child among them. And he said: 'Truly I tell
> you, unless you change and become like little
> children, you will never enter the kingdom of

heaven. Therefore, whoever takes the lowly position of this child is the greatest in the kingdom of heaven. And whoever welcomes one such child in my name welcomes me.'"

Where do we go wrong? As we discussed previously, as a child grows up and amasses more information and cultural clues, God's Spirit begins to slip away. The dark forces of the world draw us in, and soon the love we experienced being close to God in early childhood gives way to fear. If we put fear on one end of a pendulum and God's love on the other end, we can see that for centuries the pendulum has sat on the fear side. But God's love is no comparison for the darkness of fear. When we connect our Spirit/Soul with God's Spirit, the pendulum swings back to love. Relationships between humans who are connected to God are based on mutual love for each other. These relationships survive because of that mutual respect and the recognition that God is the connecting force between them.

Our world is based on the fear of others who are different from us. They may have a different culture or religion from us, and they are competing with us for supposedly scarce resources. All the religions of the world cannot fix the fear problem until we, as the world's population, become like a little child and let God connect with us. It's not "them against us," but "them with us," with God in the middle and through us all. We all have free will to make our life choices, but who would want to live in fear rather than love for their entire lifetime? It's time to recapture our youthful connection with God.

Chapter 13

God Communicates

For thousands of years, God has tried to communicate with humans. He started with the first man and woman and has continued ever since. God is alive and well. He carried on two-way communications with the Patriarchs of the Old Testament. God often has to get our attention so that we know it's really Him when He reaches out, and He often does this in rather remarkable ways. In Exodus 3, God got Moses' attention through a burning bush that never burnt up. Through the bush, He spoke to Moses:

> I have indeed seen the misery of my people in Egypt … So I have come down to rescue them from the hand of the Egyptians and to bring them up out of that land into a good and spacious land, a land flowing with milk and honey … So now, go. I am sending you to Pharaoh

to bring my people the Israelites out of Egypt.
(Exodus 3:7–8, 10)

Many of us doubt if we can serve God to His high standard. What we fail to realize is that God cannot only help us with the task at hand, but He gives us the tools to do the job. God never asks a person to do something He has not equipped him/her to do.

How do we know when God is trying to communicate with us? Think of the boy Samuel who heard a voice in the night and thought it was his master, Eli, calling him. When it happened more than once, Eli knew it was God who was trying to communicate with Samuel, so he gave Samuel instructions to respond directly to God. Sometimes we think God communicates only through other people, such as priests or other people of God. From the example of Samuel, we learn that God speaks directly to the person, and it's up to that person to respond or not. God's not likely to try to communicate with us in a burning bush, but often in ways that are unique to each person.

The prophet Elijah in the Old Testament was searching for God, and the voice of God came to him in a unique way:

> The Lord said, "Go out and stand on the mountain in the presence of the Lord, for the Lord is about to pass by." Then a great and powerful wind tore the mountains apart and shattered

the rocks before the Lord, but the Lord was not in the wind. After the wind there was an earthquake, but the Lord was not in the earthquake. And after the earthquake came a fire, but the Lord was not in the fire. And after the fire came a gentle whisper. (1 Kings 19:11–13)

Often God talks to us in that gentle whisper. Sometimes you think you're just talking to yourself, but when the message has wisdom above your knowledge, God is probably talking directly to you. At other times, God may find you in your dreams, and you wake up saying, "Where did that come from?" God may also speak to you through your intuition. I've heard many people say that their intuition guides them to do what is best for them. God is always trying to communicate with you, but often the message gets scrambled because you haven't walked through God's door to establish the total connection between Him and your Spirit/Soul.

I'd like to share my own story about how God showed me He wanted a direct connection. Thirty-five years ago, I walked through His door and opened a direct connection through my Spirit/Soul with God. Two years later, my wife collapsed at work and was taken to hospital, where she was diagnosed with a cancerous brain tumor. She was operated on twice to remove the tumor, and received radiation to kill any cancer cells that may have been missed in the operation. Having an open door to the Lord, I was in constant prayer for healing. Initially, the cancer seemed to respond to the medical work and the prayers. Her health improved, and it appeared that we'd received the miracle we'd prayed for. During one of my visits to my wife in hospital in Toronto, I visited the chapel with my teenage daughter and my wife. Prayer was obviously on all of our lips. While in the chapel, I walked to the front, climbed onto the chancel, and stood behind the pulpit. Suddenly, the front of the chapel glowed with an intense light that could only come from a divine source. My wife and daughter witnessed this in amazement. Then an angel descended from above the chancel and, without saying a word, handed me a spiritual golden sword and then disappeared, leaving us spellbound.

At the time, I was bewildered about the whole experience. Angels aren't supposed to visit humans in this day and age, but one had just visited me. After that miraculous experience, I began to search for the spiritual meaning of a sword. There are several incidents in scripture where swords are used in a physical battle, but the Apostle Paul in Ephesians 6 refers to the sword in the spiritual sense, instructing Jesus' followers to put on the armor of God to stand against the dark forces that would attack them and try to destroy their faith: "Take the helmet of salvation and the sword of the Spirit, which is the word of God" (Ephesians 6:17). This passage describes a double-edged sword meant to be my protection against the dark side, but also a tool to spread God's Word.

Revelation 19:13–15 describes an end time scenario as Jesus returns to reign and rule for a thousand years. Once again, the sword is identified as His weapon:

> He is dressed in a robe dipped in blood, and his name is the Word of God. The armies of heaven were following him, riding on white horses and dressed in fine linen, white and clean. Coming out of his mouth is a sharp sword with which to strike down the nations. He will rule with an iron scepter. On his robe and on his thigh he has this name written: KING OF KINGS AND LORD OF LORDS.

Receiving a golden sword from an angel sent a very powerful message to me that God wants to communicate with all humans. I'm just a simple vessel who has been blessed by God because I opened myself to Him.

During my wife's illness, God laid on my heart instructions to create a Christian board game that would illustrate the Christian's response to everyday situations. It was to be called Mount Zion, and the game board was to be a three-dimensional mountain that would have to be climbed to reach the Crown of Life at the top. It contained Blessing Cards to illustrate how a Christian should deal with issues and that instructed the players to move up the mountain. There were also Trial Cards that illustrated the wrong way of dealing with situations. These moved the player down the mountain. The cards were also biblically referenced. There were also Prayer Cards and Gifts of the Spirit Cards that enhanced the player's journey.

God gave me the design of the game, which took me from a prototype through to the construction of the entire game, including packaging. I'd like to share the experience of creating the 150 Blessing Cards and the 150 Trial Cards. God led me to create the Blessing Cards in the middle of my late wife's illness, recuperation, and eventual death. How does one write blessings in a crisis such as I was going through? God was obviously working through me in what can only be described as His writing and not mine. When I'd sit down to draft what was to be written on a card, it was as if I stepped aside and the information flowed through my hand out onto the page. The same thing happened after my wife's death when the Trial Cards were written. Why in the world would God communicate with me through the creation of a Christian board game? I still wrestle with that question to this day. What was God trying to accomplish? Was He trying to heal me through this process? After a year of trying to market the game with limited success, I stopped. While God communicated with and through me for two years, only a few people played the game. I often wonder about the process He led me through *(See Appendix A)*.

Did God stop communicating with me when I finished creating it? I didn't have any communication from God that

I was to market the game at that time. I just assumed that I was supposed to take it to the world myself. Often God will communicate with us, but our execution of His direction or instructions may be at some future time. We must always remember that time does not exist in heaven. I thought God worked in our time zone, and I'd often run ahead of God, thinking I was doing what He wanted. Eventually I'd find out that I wasn't on God's timetable.

I only have a couple of the games left in my possession, but for all I know, God may want people to play it today or even ten years from now. Probably it will be played some day as an electronic game on a laptop or tablet. Only God knows, and He certainly hasn't communicated that message to me. Maybe it was just meant for me to come to grips with a very challenging time in my life. All I know is that God gave me the response to my wife's death when I got the call one morning on the way to work that she had passed. I broke into tears, because even though I knew the time was close for her death, it still hit me like a sledge hammer. Through the tears, I thanked God for giving her to me for twenty years as a gift. From that day on, God has shown me that every person who enters my life is a gift. Some are only with us as an acquaintance for a very short time, some are with us as family and friends or co-workers for longer periods of time, and some are with us for a lifetime. Regardless of the time, all are gifts from God. Some may be a pain in you know where, but everyone you meet is a reflection of what you need to know in your own life. God works in mysterious ways, but be assured that God is alive and well and is trying to communicate with you.

Chapter 14

Why Do Bad Things Happen to Good People?

The book of Job is probably one of the most relatable books in the Old Testament to us today as we try to come to grips with the many challenges we face in our lives. Most of us are challenged by many events in our lives that we wish we didn't have to endure, but we do endure and eventually come out of them. Some of us may be at the beginning of a crisis, others in the middle of a crisis, and some coming out the other side. You can't live a full life on this earth without experiencing crises, difficulties, or challenges. In my own life, I've experienced many crises, but the one that stands out for me is my first wife's brain cancer and the helplessness I felt when prayers didn't produce a lasting miracle. Watching a loved one go through two brain surgeries and radiation, and feeling like you've lived in a hospital yourself for months on end, you question life's very existence. Watching my loved one ebb away in a thirteen-week coma is a crisis that I survived, and my faith in God grew in strength rather than diminishing to a rejection of our Lord.

Few biblical texts reveal the true nature of God as well as the forty-two chapters of the book of Job in the Old Testament. Often when bad things happen to us, we try to shift the blame from ourselves to others, and often we blame God when it looks like He's exacting punishment or revenge on us for some sin we've committed. Let's look at Job and try to place ourselves in his shoes. Job went through those same types of challenges. In our day, Job would be a billionaire. He owned a massive farm with thousands of animals. He had a wonderful family with seven sons and four daughters and, wonder of wonders, they got along with each other beautifully. On birthdays, they got together to celebrate each other. Job was a man of faith and was highly respected in his community. Everyone came to him for advice, and because of his faith in God, his counsel was held in very high regard.

God also loved Job for his faith and his determination to live a righteous life according to the Law of Moses. But behind the scenes a conversation took place that Job was not privy to. God was holding Job up as an example for all mankind. Satan challenged God to take away the protection he was giving to Job. God had as much faith in Job as Job had in God, so he let Satan take away everything that mattered to Job. First, Job lost all his earthly possessions, and then his sons and daughters were all killed when a tornado (we assume) hit their home. Even with all this disaster, he hung on to his faith in God: "Naked I came from my mother's womb, and naked I will depart. The Lord gave and the Lord has taken away; may the name of the Lord be praised" (Job 1:21).

Wow! If this happened to you, could you say the same? Well, Satan came back to try one more time to get Job to give up his faith in God. This time Job got a serious skin infection that was very, very painful and covered his entire body. He was in total agony, and he cursed the day of his birth, wishing he'd either never been born or that he'd been stillborn. He even considered suicide in Job 3. By this point, Job's wife had lost her faith and told him to curse God and die.

Prior to these crises, Job had been the one to give advice to others. Well, now the tables were turned, and his friends decided to give him advice. What was even worse was that Job no longer had the respect of the people in his own community. Isn't it amazing that we tend to hold in high regard people who are recognized for the wealth they've amassed–our sports stars, film stars, and music stars—but average people who go through crises and disasters are often never recognized for their greatness and faithfulness?

At this point in this message, we must remember that it was not God who brought this disaster on Job. When problems befall us, we have friends who want to commiserate with us and help us get past our misery. Job had four friends who came to support him in his time of need. These were friends he'd known for years, and he felt they had an understanding of his circumstances and would be able to help him.

The first friend to speak was Eliphaz. His first statement to Job was, "Anyone innocent never perishes. Only the evil doers sow trouble and reap it. Man is born into trouble. I would appeal to God; I would lay my cause before Him. God saves those who need saving. God is in control of everything."

Job responds that God has it in for him: "Do I have any power to help myself? Show me where I have been wrong. Is there any wickedness on my lips?" Job then throws out a question to God. "If I have sinned, what have I done to you?"

Job's second friend, Bildad, thinks it's time to jump in. He states that God is judge and jury of mankind: "Does God pervert justice? When your children sinned against God, they received the penalty of their sins." None of his friends change Job's opinions. Once again, he asks: "How do mortals prove their innocence before God? How can I find words to argue with Him? He destroys both the blameless and the wicked." At this point, Job believes God is vengeful and doesn't play fair. Once again, I remind you that things between heaven and earth aren't always what they seem to be. God didn't bring this catastrophe on Job, but Job can only see what Job can see.

Job's third friend, Zophar, berates him: "Stop your ranting. You can't even fathom the mysteries of God. Job, you have sinned and won't accept that you have."

As you can see, Job isn't buying what his friends are putting forward as explanations for his predicament. Job still believes he did nothing wrong. He says to his friends: "You smear me with lies. You are worthless physicians, all of you! How many wrongs and sins have I committed? Show me my offense and my sins." Job still thinks it's God who is causing problems for everyone.

Eliphaz chips in and says: "Your own mouth condemns you. You have no wisdom." Even though Job thinks God is the reason for his misery, he believes God is still his friend and hangs onto his faith.

Bildad comes back at him again and states: "People like you have been caught in nets of evil and sin, and you don't really know God at all." Zophar jumps in and adds that God is vengeful, and the wicked will get swept away.

Job's thoughts turn to a more global perspective. "Why do the wicked grow old, increase in power, and die in peace?" With that question, he blows a hole in his friends' arguments.

Eliphaz responds, "Submit to the Lord and be restored if you get rid of your wickedness."

By chapter 23, Job has given up on his friends to help him through this crisis. Now he turns directly to God to state his case, but he can't find Him. He asks, "Why does the Almighty not set times for judgment?" Once again, Job is treating God as if He was a human being, like a judge in a court. He has failed to see the Lord as the Spirit of all creation. He goes on to say, "I will maintain my innocence and never let go of it."

Like most of us in a crisis, Job looks back in his life to when things were great, and he wishes for the return of the good old days. He searches for when, if ever, he may have sinned and forgotten about it, but nothing comes to mind.

Job's fourth friend, a younger man named Elihu, addresses Job: "God repays everyone for what they have done; they get what they deserve. God is judge of all. You say, 'I am in the right and not God.' Your wickedness only affects humans." Elihu tries to speak on behalf of God. "If humans obey and serve the Lord, they will spend their days in prosperity and their years in contentment."

Once again, things in heaven and on earth are not what they seem to be. God wasn't the author of Job's problems. The arguments put forth by Job and his four friends didn't come from an understanding of the full picture. Often we speak about things that are not rooted in truth, thinking that we have the whole picture when we only have a piece of the information.

In chapter 40, we hear from God as He addresses Job's warped and incomplete view of himself in the world: "Where were you when I laid the earth's foundations? Will the one who contends with the Almighty correct Him? Let him who accuses God answer Him. Would you discredit my justice? Would you condemn me to justify yourself? Who has a claim against me that I must repay? Everything under heaven belongs to me."

Job is brought up short by the words of the Lord. He has been shown the total picture of heaven and earth. He now understands his place in God's creation, and he simply says:

> I know you can do all things; no purpose of yours can be thwarted. You asked, "Who is this that obscures my plans without knowledge?" Surely I spoke of things I did not understand, things too wonderful for me to know. You said, "Listen now and I will speak; I will question you and you shall answer me." My ears have heard you but now my eyes have seen you. Therefore I despise myself and repent in dust and ashes. (Job 42:2–6)

In the end, Job's friends were also admonished and asked Job's forgiveness for not speaking the truth. The rest of Job's life was as it was in the beginning, with seven new sons and three daughters and twice the number of animals for his farm.

Let's remember that Job lived according to the Laws of Moses and believed he was righteous in the eyes of the Law. We see now that he didn't have the entire picture of how God operates in His creation. The Apostle Paul in Galatians admonished the Galatian church for its failure to move beyond the Law to live a life of faith according to Jesus Christ's teachings. How is your faith? Have you seen the true nature of God? Without a true connection with the Lord, we will rely on friends' advice and fail to see the true God of the universe and follow the teachings of his Son, Jesus Christ.

Chapter 15

God through Humans

God is love, and the Spirit/Soul of humans is also love. There can be no dichotomy between God and the image He gave to all humans. Wow! That certainly doesn't sound like many of the people we meet today. Many are wrapped up in their own lives with little thought about the people around them, including their immediate families. How can people be so vindictive and nasty to others when a piece of God's Spirit of love resides in them? It comes back to the free choice that God has given to each of us and how we choose to live the life we've been given. The human ego often stands between people and God, and self-preservation is its most important attribute; however, God didn't intend the human ego to be in the driver's seat of our lives. His Spirit was supposed to reign supreme in every person's life.

Throughout the Bible, we see many examples of God infusing His Spirit into humans. In Exodus 31:3, God tells Moses about the gifts He's given to Bezalel, a metallurgist:

"I have filled him with the Spirit of God, with wisdom, with understanding, with knowledge and with all kinds of skills." He offers us the same attributes today when we are in total connection with Him:

> No one has ever seen God; but if we love one another, God lives in us and his love is made complete in us. This is how we know that we live in Him and He in us: He has given us of his Spirit. We have seen and testify that the Father has sent his Son to be the Savior of the world. If anyone acknowledges that Jesus is the Son of God, God lives in them and they in God. And so we know and rely on the love God has for us. (1 John 4:12–16)

For thousands of years, we have worshiped God from afar. Since He has been invisible to us, we've relied on our faith to bring Him alive in our own lives. That is beginning to change as we recognize that God is alive and well and a breath away from us at all times. He's not only all around us, but resides in us continually. In Acts 2:17–21, the Apostle Peter quotes the prophet Joel from the Old Testament, recognizing this aspect of God with us and in us:

> In the last days, God says, I will pour out my Spirit on all people. Your sons and daughters will

prophesy, your young men will see visions, your old men will dream dreams. Even on my servants, both men and women, I will pour out my Spirit in those days, and they will prophesy. I will show wonders in the heavens above and signs on the earth below, blood and fire and billows of smoke. The sun will be turned to darkness and the moon to blood, before the coming of the great and glorious day of the Lord. And everyone who calls on the name of the Lord will be saved.

Once again, we have the free choice God gave us, but the true nature of God will shine through humans. We will be recognized as sons and daughters of God, just as Jesus was recognized as the Son of God. He's not just looking for one Son anymore, but He wants millions of sons and daughters around the world. We are entering a period of time in which God wants to be the Father/Mother God of all humankind, not just the chosen few. The prophet Ezekiel describes not only the return of Israel to their homeland, but God's work in us in the twenty-first century:

I will give them an undivided heart and put a new spirit in them; I will remove from them their heart of stone and give them a heart of flesh. Then they will follow my decrees and be careful to keep my laws. They will be my people, and I will be their God. (Ezekiel 11:19–20)

This raises a profound question. How can we treat other people with the same Spirit of God in them so wretchedly? We abuse our neighbors with words and actions that can only be described as despicable. It's almost as if we don't even recognize that they are a part of us and we are a part of them. Jesus highlights this in a conversation with a Pharisee:

> "Teacher, which is the greatest commandment of the Law?" Jesus replied: "Love the Lord your God with all your heart and with all your soul and with all your mind. This is the first and greatest commandment. And the second is like it: Love your neighbor as yourself. All the Law and the Prophets hang on these two commandments." (Matthew 22:36–40)

Jesus makes it clear that we all have a piece of God's Spirit of Love in us, and we must honor everyone's Spirit, as we would honor our own Spirit.

This brings us to the question of how to relate to people who are not like us. They may have a different religion or a different culture or a different skin color. Many people who are different from us are foreign, and we have little, if anything, in common with them. What we fail to do is look at them as Jesus did. He saw everyone from the same perspective as God, and we should too. The only way you can look at every other person as Jesus instructed is through that pure connection we can establish between our Spirit/Soul and God. Furthermore, unless a person tells or shows you their religion and culture, you'll have no knowledge of their true nature, which is God's Spirit in them, just as He is in you.

The color of people's skin has divided people for centuries; often, slavery was used to subjugate one race of people to another. If you removed the skin of every person on earth, you'd be confronted with bone, sinew, and flesh. How would you even know where they lived or worshiped, or what their culture was like? Most of the evils of this world do not result from differences, as we would like to think, but from people seeking power and dominion over others. So many wars throughout history demonstrate the opposite of what Jesus commanded. Enemies became less than equal, and often were portrayed as subhuman. Regardless of how different our neighbors are in culture, race, sexual orientation, or religion, we are all still a part of God, and He of us. Those who would attempt to divide us are not connected to God; however, they are still our neighbors, and our love for them must be equal to those who are like us.

As you look around, do you see anyone who looks exactly like you? Even twins and triplets believe they are in some way different from the other. The beauty of the human race is that we're all different in some way from everyone else. We all have the Spirit of God in us, but we're also walking our own individual paths on this earth. How can we be a piece of God yet be totally different in appearance, personality, emotions, belief systems, and experiences? This is the mystery of why God made us all so differently.

I have my own theory on this, and I can share it with you. I believe the Creator God is constantly learning, and His Spirit grows through our experiences when we incarnate on earth. Remember, when we pass over in death, our Spirit returns to God, and our experiences, memories, and love bring new creations and understandings to Him as He develops new multiverses. You could almost say we are God's eyes and ears on earth, and He needs us just as we need Him. We are all equal in God's eyes, and we are expected to treat every other person as we want to be treated ourselves. There are some very despicable people on this earth, but we must remember that they too have a piece of God's Spirit in them as well—it's just not connected to God. When you have a pure connection with God, praying for those who are despicable is just as easy as praying for your friends. That is how Jesus did it, and it's how we can do it also. The Apostle Paul describes how people who are different from each other can come together as one body with that connection to God:

> Just as a body, though one, has many parts, but all its many parts, form one body, so it is with Christ. For we were all baptized by one Spirit,

so as to form one body—whether the Jews or Gentiles, slave or free—and we were all given the one Spirit to drink. Even so the body is not made up of one part, but of many. Now if the foot should say, "Because I am not a hand, I do not belong to the body," it would not for that reason stop being part of the body. And if the ear should say, "Because I am not an eye I do not belong to the body," it would not for that reason stop being part of the body. If the whole body were an eye, where would the sense of hearing be? If the whole body were an ear where would the sense of smell be? But in fact God has placed the parts in the body, every one of them, just as he wanted them to be. If they were all one part where would the body be? As it is, there are many parts, but one body. (1 Corinthians 12:12–20)

Our differences have driven us apart for thousands of years. When we finally recognize that we are all different but the same in Spirit, we can begin to heal our differences and live as God meant us to from the very beginning in the Garden of Eden. In the end, God gives us the opportunity to join our Spirit/Soul with His to live as Christ taught us when He was here on the earth. The choice is ours and ours alone. God will never force us to do anything, but the reward of joining Him is incalculatable.

Chapter 16

God Answers Prayers

*T*hroughout history, humans have wanted to talk to God. The problem is, we can't see God, so we throw our words out, hoping He may hear them and answer in some fashion. Most times it feels as though we throw our words on the wind, and they are carried to who knows where. Every religion that recognizes one God has a ritual of prayers, hoping that at least some will be answered. The Bible is rife with instructions on how to communicate with God through prayer. It must be important to be mentioned in scripture 108 times. The Christian church even has elements of prayer: praise, thanksgiving, confession, and intercession. However, the communication with God seems to be one-sided when we pray.

Even though prayer feels one-sided, humans continue unabated praying to a God they cannot see. Even Jesus was asked how a person should pray to God, and we now have the Lord's Prayer, found in Matthew 6:9–13, with a shorter version in Luke 11:2–4. Let's take a moment to understand what Jesus was saying when He gave His followers that well-known prayer.

"Our father in heaven, hallowed be your name." In the first line, Jesus asks us to recognize the Creator God of all things, including us, and indicates where we can find Him. Unfortunately, finding heaven is a problem for most people. We know that God is omnipresent, and heaven isn't a place, but a location for the entirety of God Himself/Herself.

"Your kingdom come, your will be done on earth as it is in Heaven." Jesus preached about the Kingdom of God in His ministry, and we can envisage peace on earth and the utopia of an earth filled with God's Love. That line in the Lord's Prayer is our plea to God to see that beautiful kingdom not just in heaven as it is now, but as it will exist on the earth as well.

"Give us our daily bread." We sometimes forget to recognize that even the food we eat is a gift from God. The Creator not only created every plant on earth, but His intention is to supply all of our needs, including what we eat.

"Forgive us our debts (sins) as we have forgiven our debtors (or those who have sinned against us)." This is our instruction for creating positive relationships with everyone around us. It is simply to forgive and seek forgiveness.

"And lead us not into temptation, but deliver us from evil." The dark side of our nature and our ego can lead us down paths that are contrary to the light God wants us to follow. In this final line, we ask God to be our guide in this lifetime. He is instructing us to connect with His Spirit, so that our way through this life can be in His Light and Love.

The Bible contains many encouragements to pray to God, but is there a relationship with Him that we must have for prayers to be answered? Proverbs 15:29 gives us some indication: "The Lord is far from the wicked, but he hears the prayer of the righteous." Jesus instructed His followers in the power of prayer and its results in Matthew 21:21–22:

> Truly I tell you, if you have faith and do not doubt, not only can you do what was done to the fig tree, but also you can say to this mountain, "Go throw yourself into the sea," and it will be done. If you believe, you will receive whatever you ask for in prayer.

Most of us look at that passage and say, "Really?" But when you connect God's Spirit with your Spirit/Soul, the command to dump a mountain into the sea may not be as far-fetched as you might initially think. Jesus tells each of us that the power God can give us through prayer is phenomenal, and we need to find out how to use that prayer in our daily lives to not only influence our own lives, but the lives of those around us and around the world. The Apostle Paul advises: "Rejoice always, pray continually, give thanks in all circumstances; for this is God's will for you in Christ Jesus" (1 Thessalonians 5:16–18).

The instructions for prayer are very clear. When we connect with God, we want to hear His instructions and guidance for every moment of our life. This can only be achieved by considering His wishes for us and not just our own. What does it mean to pray and have our prayers heard and responded to by God? James advises us that prayers must be based in faith:

> Is anyone among you in trouble? Let them pray. Is
> anyone among you sick? Let them call the elders
> of the church to pray over them, and anoint them
> with oil in the name of the Lord. And the prayer
> offered in faith will make the sick person well;
> the Lord will raise them up. If they have sinned,
> they will be forgiven. Therefore, confess your sins
> to each other and pray for each other so that you
> may be healed. The prayer of a righteous person
> is powerful and effective. (James 5:13–16)

In biblical times and throughout the last two thousand years, the elders of the church were expected to be in direct connection with God. Since the average person had little education, the authorities in the church were the few who supposedly had the connection with God to pray for healing or forgiveness. Unfortunately, many elders in the church may have learned about God through the scriptures, but they had no real spiritual connection with Him. Jude adds an additional dimension to prayer beyond faith: "But you, dear friends, by building yourself up in your most holy faith, and praying in the Holy Spirit, keep yourselves in God's love as you wait for the mercy of our Lord Jesus Christ to bring you to eternal life" (Jude 20–21).

Praying in the Holy Spirit raises an even bigger question for us. How do we pray in the Holy Spirit? The Apostle Paul also insisted on this: "And pray in the Spirit on all occasions with all kinds of prayers and requests" (Ephesians 6:18a).

Let's take some time to think about what praying means for us. In our church services, most prayers that are spoken are beautiful pieces of prose and poetry. They are given in faith, but do they meet the criteria of being prayed in the Holy Spirit? Most prayers that are uttered come from the mind. Our languages are constructed in the left brain, but are the prayers that come from this part of the brain spoken in faith and through the Holy Spirit? This brings us back to who God and the Holy Spirit really are. We know God is pure love; however, humans are not just made up of half a brain. We also have a right side of the brain, which controls our emotions… and love is part of it. All the aesthetic things in life are controlled by the right brain. This includes art, music, love, and even hate. When we pray in faith, we must not only use the left side of the brain, but we must also engage the right side to enlist the Spirit of God in communication.

Words aren't enough to communicate with God. We must also enlist right brain functions. The right brain creates things such as art work, music, dancing, and multiple original concepts and activities. Every creation comes out of a vision of what the end is going to look like. Our minds are constantly visualizing how we see events in our lives playing out. Sometimes our visualizations are positive, and sometimes they could be quite destructive for ourselves or others if brought to realization. When we connect our Spirit/Soul to the Spirit of God, the visualizations can become reality. This is where the power of God enters our world through us, and it's what Jesus was referring to when He said that if His followers had the faith and prayed through the Holy Spirit, they could visualize a mountain being moved into the ocean. Now, we know our prayer abilities have a long way to go before we can produce that miracle. There are people in this world today who have developed a pure connection with God and can create miracles in nature.

How can a person pray in faith and in the Holy Spirit? Prayer must come from both the left and right side of the brain. Our prayers are usually left brain in origin, and we neglect the creative side of our nature. When we pray in the Spirit, we have to create an image in our mind to illustrate how the outcome of the prayer should appear. For example, when we pray for a person who is sick, we ask God to heal that person. But what image do you have of that person? Do you see them as they are now, or do you imagine a totally healthy person? God, who is love, communicates with us not only through our words, but through the creative side of the brain. Prayers need to send the message of the expected end result. We are a piece of God, and it's only natural that God would respond to our prayers through our Spirit/Soul. This brings us back to our relationship with God through that direct connection we have with Him. If we really want to see miracles from our prayers, we need that pure connection with God that Jesus and many others have throughout history. We have the same spirit of God in us that Jesus and the apostles had, and we can be fully human as they were.

Chapter 11

God Is a Change Advocate

Have you ever taken a few minutes to close your eyes and let the visions of the past flow into your mind? When I do this, I like to dwell on what it was like to be a child growing up in southern Ontario in the mid-1940s, 50s, and 60s. Very pleasant visions come to mind. I remember sitting on a stool beside the old wood fire while talking to my mother for hours on end. I had to know everything. Why did this happen? Why are we doing this? What does this mean? Why? Why? Why? I must have driven my mother nuts; however, she was a very caring person who answered all of my questions ... well, almost all of them.

The questions that come to mind the most concern why my father farmed the way he did. I remember saying to my father: "Why don't we plow up that whole field? It's not producing any good crops. That hay crop isn't yielding much anymore. Why don't you let me work it up and put in some grain?"

Every time I brought up the subject, my father would say, "No, no, we're not going to do that." I never understood why he wouldn't let me plow that field. My mother gave me the answer one day as I sat there on the stool talking to her. She reminded me that my father almost lost the farm during the Great Depression of the 1930s. According to her, that was why my father never took any chances on the farm. I knew my father was a very adventuresome young man when he was young. I was told that when he bought the farm, he had all sorts of grand ideas about what he wanted to do with it. But what happened in the meantime? It's the same question society today is confronted with when we face change. Why should I change? Every day we're confronted with the same thing. But what is our response? What is your response?

Having spent my entire life in education, you'd think I'd have a lot to say on this topic. Well, I have! My first shock as a student came at the beginning of my first year in high school. As I mentioned previously, I attended a one-room school house with twenty students in the 1950s, which seems like an eternity ago. After Grade 8, I moved to a small high school in the nearby town. There were 120 students in Grade 9. I remember the principal addressing us on the first day of school. He was a blunt man who had served his country like so many of my other teachers who served in World War II. He was austere and didn't beat around the bush when he wished to impart some of his wisdom to us. He stood before the 120 Grade 9 students and made a profound statement:

"Look around you. Only 10 percent of you will graduate from high school." That had a major impact on me. As I looked around at the rest of my peers, I promised myself that I'd be in that 10 per cent. Well, lo and behold, when I graduated from high school, only twelve students out of the 120 walked across the stage to get a diploma. Graduation rates are higher today, with an average of almost four out of five students receiving a diploma; however, if you're aboriginal or from certain minorities, you have half the chance of graduating than a white student.

The change in graduation rates over the past fifty years appears on the surface to be quite remarkable. The issue is not how many young people graduate, but what have they learned along the way? We often laughed that you would study like mad for a final exam to show how much you learned, but then a week later most of the knowledge was forgotten. If you had to write that exam again, you'd fail miserably. What really is the purpose of education?

In the 1800s, with the rise of the Industrial Revolution, children could no longer be expected to work from an early age to support their families. In a society that prided itself on being civilized, such child labor was deemed inappropriate. Education became the means to moving children and young people out of the workforce and out of the homes with the express purpose of controlling them for at least eight years of their life. Today that has stretched into twelve to sixteen years. If you tested a group of young adults on what they've learned over those many years, you'd find that most can read to a certain level, compute some mathematics, and quote a few facts, but research has shown that most of what one would consider important could probably be learned in a fraction of the time spent in formal education. Obviously, this would be hypothetical, but I think I have many who agree with me on this issue.

This comes back to the present question: What is the importance of an education today? Education systems around the world are established on history and are not forward thinking about what a child should learn to live and work in the world of tomorrow. Those who make the decisions about what is taught in schools today probably graduated with their own diplomas in the twentieth century, so they pattern today's system after what was taught to them as students. Most were taught a specific curriculum created by those who were educated in the 1950s and 1960s. Do you see where I'm going with this? Education has always been patterned after the previous generation and never with a view to the future. As students themselves, those in charge of education planning today were taught a specific curriculum for each subject and then tested on it to see what they had learned. These educational planners believe the same process is important for today's youth. They know that students will quickly forget what they study for exams, but they have no answer to this problem except to do more of the same. Albert Einstein said that the definition of insanity is doing the same thing over and over and expecting a different outcome. I could probably write a book on why education hasn't change in 150 years, but I'll keep that for another time.

After a career spanning thirty-six years as a school principal in eight public schools, and teaching some university courses, I can claim to have worked with thousands of students from the ages of four to twenty-two years of age, and I enjoyed their growth over those many years. I've observed that children are changing in ways that many educators have difficulty relating to. When I was growing up and during my early years as an educator, students saw the teacher as an authority figure who knew everything about a topic. Discipline was by both fear and respect, with some educators relying more on one than the other. What I find interesting today is that the fear is gone, and so is the teacher as the all-knowing expert. Students today aren't buying into the curriculum being fed to them. They're not the linear thinkers of the past, but have become conceptual thinkers who want to solve problems and use their creative abilities. Educational planners are saying to students: "We know what's best for you to know, and you shouldn't question us."

We're beginning to see the results of such short-sighted thinking, as students tune out, disconnect, and drop out of a school system to which they can no longer relate. I predict that if education planners around the world don't start changing the way they develop curriculum and methodologies, there will be push back by students expecting their education system to respond to their needs. Where does God fit into the picture of the future of education? God is a God of change, and much as we don't like change, education must address the issue of educating the whole child.

I believe I've been a proponent of change over the years. From wanting to plow that field to becoming a school principal at the age of twenty-three, I was Mr. Change. But I didn't understand change. I didn't understand what people go through on the road to change. I believed that everybody could change given the right circumstances, but life experiences put people on a very defensive path, and change becomes fear. Change hit my father so hard in his thirties that he had no room to take chances in the 1950s and 60s. I spent thirty-six years as school principal trying to figure out why we wrote curriculum and then asked teachers to implement it without question. Then I'd see it not being implemented as it was written. In change, we ask people to embrace the new and forget the old. But it doesn't work. I saw curriculum collecting dust on shelves. Why do some things change fairly easily, while other things don't change no matter what people do?

The puzzle of change has dogged me for most of my life. For a year in a school in Northern Ontario I was the coordinator of an Ontario government-funded Excellence in Learning Project that experimented with new ideas about teaching children. For the first time in my long career as an educator, I saw children really learning and feeling proud of their work. I saw children lining up at their teacher's door at 7:30 each morning to come in to work on whatever project the teacher had assigned. By 9:00 a.m., every child was in that classroom. I can only describe it as bees in a bee hive. Everyone was working on what they needed and wanted to do. What drove those children can only be described as CREATIVITY. These children were tapping into the very essence of God.

God is a Creator, and with a piece of Him in each of us, we too were born to be creators. So why aren't we all exhibiting a huge amount of "creator" in our own lives? Think of infants and young children who spend hours building structures out of bricks and blocks, or think of a little child's painting. Its subject may not be obvious to us, but it's totally understood by the child. As children grow up, the school experience, which has become exclusively left brain oriented, denigrates the right brain creative side that deals with cultural activities such as music, dance, art, and other creative ventures.

Currently, the arts are taking a back seat to the language, mathematics, and science elements of education. How much music is even taught in our schools today? When cuts come in budgets, the first program to go is the arts. Even the way we evaluate the various programs slants toward the left-brain-courses, with no equal weighting given to the affective subjects. God didn't intend for us to be only half educated, or to live our lives using only half our brain power. Look at a child solving a math problem and a child engaged in a creative activity. Which one has the smile on his or her face? God cannot be alive and well in our lives without the full use of our whole body, and that includes both sides of our brain.

God is the Creator of all things, and we are created in His image as creators. When we connect our Spirit/Soul with God's Spirit, we connect to His full creative powers. The future of the world rests with children who can freely use their creative powers. Children are closer to God than anyone on earth, as Jesus pointed out in Mark 10:15: "Truly I tell you, anyone who will not receive the kingdom of God like a little child will never enter it." God doesn't want us to stifle a child's learning, but to use the Spirit of Creativity He gave to each of us. The Apostle Paul reveals God's desire for the children:

> For the creation awaits in eager expectation for the children of God to be revealed. For the creation was subjected to frustration, not by its own choice, but by the will of the one who subjected it, in the hope that the creation itself will be liberated from its bondage to decay and brought into freedom and glory of the children of God. (Romans 8:19–21)

Our challenge is to raise and teach our children in the light and love of God.

Chapter 18
God in Our Emotions

As we discussed previously, the entire universe is composed of unseen light energy that exists everywhere. God uses this light energy to create all things. Just as we can't visually see microwaves or electrical waves or even magnetic waves, we are only beginning to build microscopes and digital equipment to see this light energy that we call quantum mechanics.

God is the Great Physicist. We've always thought that God and science were totally separate, but Albert Einstein developed a theory that totally debunked the accepted Newtonian physics theory that everything should be examined from a purely physical perspective. In other words, if you can't see it and prove it, it doesn't exist. That philosophy has guided almost everything we do in life. "Prove it" is its standard. This leads us to only see the world through our five senses. It's an easy way to view the world; however, we can't see electricity or X-rays, but we still believe they exist because of the results of using of them. We can't see electricity, but we do see the light bulb that glows with white light and brightens the room. The same is true with X-rays—we can't see them, but we can see the picture of a person's internal body on film or in a digital image.

As previously discussed, nearly a century has gone by since Einstein gave us his famous $E = MC^2$, which means: E (ENERGY) = M (MATTER/MASS) X (times) C^2 (SPEED OF LIGHT (186,000 miles per second) (SQUARED). How did Einstein and several other scientists come up with this bizarre statement that everything is made of energy? The following is their belief in how it all functions: The atom is a basic unit of five that consists of a dense central _nucleus_ surrounded by a _cloud_ of _negatively charged electrons_. The _atomic nucleus_ contains a mix of positively charged _protons_ and electrically neutral _neutrons_. With this in mind, they concluded that every living thing is made up of atoms. Quantum physicists discovered that physical atoms are made up of vortices of energy that are constantly spinning and vibrating like a spinning top, radiating unique energy signatures. Albert Einstein recognized that energy and matter are one and the same. Since atoms come together to make up the cells of a human body, we can conclude that we are massive energy systems. Just one cell in our bodies contains millions of atoms and the DNA molecule of life itself. Every DNA molecule contains the knowledge to reproduce itself as a new human being. Just to add to this mind-boggling information, we have fifty trillion cells in our body, and these cells come together to form bones, muscles, organs, skin, a nervous system, and much more. While scientists work hard to clone and reproduce life in artificial intelligence, they just don't have all the pieces of the puzzle. The more you consider how complex the human body is, the more you realize that only a God who is alive and well can reproduce us and keep us healthy.

How can a person stay healthy for an entire lifetime with such a complex structure? Western medicine over the last century has tried to learn everything it can about the human body and how it functions. The pharmaceutical industry has grown out of this approach to keeping the human body healthy. This approach relies on viewing the body as a machine that can be manipulated through chemical means. The drug industry has become a major force in the medical profession and is based on chemicals eliminating, or at least reducing, health problems. The big drug companies have been accused of keeping people sick instead of eliminating diseases in order to keep the profits flowing in.

Even though Newtonian physics has been proven to be ineffective in eliminating disease in the body, the effort by scientists to further the common-sense approach that Albert Einstein advocated continues down a path that has proven itself to be inadequate for the twenty-first century health of humans. For centuries, Asian medicine has gone beyond dealing with the health of humans' physical bodies. These practitioners knew that the human body was more than what could be seen, so they looked for the problems of disease behind the visible and dealt with varying approaches to the energy fields of the human body. Medical procedures such as acupuncture have crept into Western healthcare, but mainstream Western medicine remains grounded in an archaic view of how the human body operates.

Those who are experimenting with energy will become the new face of medicine over the next few years. Previously, we have discussed to a limited extent how God created the human body in His image. We know we've been given a piece of God's Spirit as our Spirit/Soul, and it resides in us throughout our lifetime and for all time with the Creator God. We are eternal when we think about who we are with God. We were there with Him when He formed the universe, our galaxy, our solar system, and our earth. We will also be with Him to the end of time, if time even exists in heaven.

Let's look at how God created us as physical bodies in more detail. Biologists inform us that every cell in our bodies is an electromagnetic entity that can receive energy from other sources, but it's also capable of sending messages to every other cell in the body. Cells can also send quantum energy outside the body to distant receivers. On the outside of each cell are thousands of receptors and transmitters of this energy. Cellular biologists have also discovered that removing the nucleus from a cell doesn't kill the cell, but if the outside membrane of the cell is removed, the cell will die. From that discovery, they have concluded that the outer covering membrane of the cell is really a mini-brain. We have the brain in our head that controls our subconscious and conscious actions, but we also have fifty trillion brains in our cells that send out and receive messages millions of times a minute. Only God could create such a complex creature as us. Even if we stopped with the physical body we could only feel awe for who God is.

Everyone wants a healthy body, and we spend considerable time praying to God for healing of this fragile instrument we call the human body. What we fail to realize is that the physical portion of us is only one quarter of our being. Our health relies not just on the parts we see, but also on the parts we don't see. These parts include our emotional body, our mental body, and our Spirit/Soul body.

The emotional body is connected to our heart and right brain functions, which control our love centers; however, the emotional body has not been well understood by the medical community, and psychiatric and chemical solutions have been applied to problems in the emotional body. Deb Shapiro in her book, *Your Body Speaks Your Mind*, explains what happens when emotional problems arise in a person:

> Psycho/Emotional Factors; emotional pain is just as real as physical pain and can be far more invasive. Long-held resentments, anger, bitterness, hurt, fear, guilt, and shame, all play their role in debilitating your energy. You may feel shame

or guilt for something you did or didn't do, or long-held resentments or anger for something that was done to you. You may feel unworthy or lacking in confidence, overcome by fear or panic, helplessness, depressed, or full of grief. You may spend many years building a wall around your heart in order to protect it from being hurt, but in so doing also wall off your own feelings of love and passion. Eventually, you become isolated, locked into separation, unable to allow for fear of being hurt, unable to forgive due to past resentment, unable to achieve success for dread of failure. All these feelings have their effect in the body: on your immune system, your blood circulation, your digestion, and so on.[1]

Failure to deal with the negative issues in your emotional body can result in devastating health issues in the physical body. Deb Shapiro says it best:

Emotions that are denied can disappear for a very long time, as denial is a large and heavy blanket. Denial enables you to convince yourself that everything is fine and no problem, when

---

1   Deb Shapiro, *Your Body Speaks Your Mind* (Boulder, CO: Sounds True, Inc. 2006), 32.

underneath the surface, if you dare look, you'll find a mass of feelings and traumas. Denied emotions can erupt. They can spill out through other emotions or strange behavior. They can cause physical difficulties, sexual problems, relationship problems, or addiction. The event itself may have gone, but the emotional impact can stay with us for many years, affecting us on the cellular level.[2]

The free will given to humans by God isn't conducive to a healthy emotional body. Experiences, both negative and positive, build up in our emotional bodies. Over the centuries, the church has declared negative energy as being sins against God, other people, or ourselves. I often refer to negative energy as "imbalanced" and the creative light energy of God as "balanced," and I will continue to refer to energy in those terms. How do imbalanced energies lodge in our emotional bodies? Deb Shapiro identified many situations that can result in a build-up of negative or imbalanced energies. Most of us grew up in homes that stressed standards of behavior that were acceptable in our communities.

What happens when we leave our communities and join communities that operate contrary to the way our parents raised us? What happens to our emotional bodies when we're

---

2   Shapiro, *Your Body Speaks Your Mind*, 36.

asked to do things or say things contrary to the belief system of our parents? Most times, in order to fit in, we do and say things that we would never say or do in front of our parents. Let's consider the example of a young man or woman who was raised in a Christian home that taught the Ten Commandments as their guide to living. Now let's put that person in the military, where they're trained to kill other humans who are labeled as "the enemy" and made to appear less than human. This training contradicts the beliefs taught in childhood. Let's take the young man or woman and put them in a combat situation, where they're expected to kill the enemy combatant. Let's take this scenario to the point of actually committing the killing. Now let's bring the young man and woman home after the war experience, where they saw people die by their hand or saw their friends die or be severely injured. Where are the images of those horrendous scenes stored?

The emotional body is a storehouse for our life experiences. It stores those images as pictures or visual clips that come to the conscious mind at any time of the day or night. Often the images pop into our heads when some memory or stimulus brings them back to the surface. At night, dreams come rushing back in as nightmares. We've discovered over the past few years that our veterans, police officers, fire fighters, and other people who've gone through a horrendous experience can develop a condition known as PTSD (Post-Traumatic Stress Disorder). If they're not cleared out of their emotional bodies, horrific images can haunt people for the rest of their lives. Counseling and drugs cannot remove horrendous images; they must be cleared out totally, and only God can help.

Imbalanced energy is like the junk we collect in our homes but can't remember why we ever accumulated it in the first place. Removing imbalanced energy in our bodies makes room for healing and the restoration of wellness. Deb Shapiro suggests to us:

> Accept yourself just as you are, with all your weaknesses, mistakes, and helplessness. You have to strip naked emotionally and start from there: bringing forgiveness to every part of your being, into your pain, into your fear, into your illness, into your shame, forgiving your childhood, forgiving yourself for being abused, the thinking you deserve to be punished or hurt, for the way you have treated others, for the guilt, for all mistakes you have made and the hopelessness you have felt. The more you forgive yourself the more you will be able to forgive others. [3]

Our approach must be a spiritual one. When we connect our Spirit/Soul with God and use the prayers suggested

---

3   Deb Shapiro, *Your Body Speaks Your Mind* (Boulder, CO: Sounds True, Inc. 2006), 95

earlier, we can ask Him to move out the imbalanced energy in our bodies and fill us with His balanced light energy.

I'd like to share an experience I had in clearing out imbalanced energy from a woman who has a Ph.D. in Psychology and had undergone a tremendous amount of abuse at the hands of her former husband, who still haunted her on a regular basis. I worked with her to clear out the imbalanced energy and called on the light energy of God to fill the void left when the negative energy had cleared out. This is her story:

"I would like to take this opportunity to give my personal testimonial regarding the incredible healing experience I encountered while partaking in Dr. Walker's Energy Balancing Sessions in May 2014. I have been a trauma psychologist for almost thirty years. Prior to meeting Dr. Walker, I was severely assaulted in March of 2014, which profoundly affected my mind, body, and soul. I had the pleasure of attending a workshop that Dr. Walker presented. The workshop was both theoretical and experiential. I can attest that not only did his theoretical presentation resonate with my belief system and the research I've done regarding Energy Healing, but also the experiential exercise had a profound effect on my symptoms of Post-Traumatic Stress Disorder. After being led through the group exercise, I felt a new sense of hope that I would heal from my ordeal. The healing meditation permutated my mind, body, soul and spirit, leaving me with the sense that I would be better than just "okay." Also, the effects were immediate! I felt that I was not only spiritually protected, but that I could also practice the exercises and transmute the negative energies around me.

"My second experience with Dr. Walker was a one-on-one session. This session consisted of a healing meditation to clear out my imbalance energy and to add a secondary "protective shield" to my being. Dr. Walker had no prior knowledge that the previous May (2013) my wrist was broken (spiral fracture) and that in August of that same year I broke two of my ribs. Intuitively, he knew where the traumatic injuries were in my body, and during the session, I could feel the residual pain leave immediately. It has been over two months since my treatment, and I haven't been affected by those injuries. His healing work has had an enigmatic effect on me and has profoundly affected my physical, mental, and spiritual perspective in a very positive way. Moreover, my twenty-one-year-old son, who was also experiencing some difficulties with stress and life transitions, underwent Dr. Walker's healing mediation, and I noted an immediate, positive change in him. I am truly indebted to Dr. Walker's treatments and his work. Injuries and old traumas that couldn't be addressed by our conventional medical community were "miraculously healed" through his research-based method of Energy Healing."

While this lady gave me permission to share her experience with everyone, I feel that announcing her name and address would not be advisable at this time. I would like to further share with you an experience I had with her about four months after the energy clearing and balancing. I met her at a meeting and was absolutely taken aback by her appearance. She looked vibrant, happy, and twenty years younger than when I'd first met her. This has to be the result of clearing out the PTSD energy and replacing it with God's light. It was truly amazing for me. God is alive and well, and He can bring back our own wellness!

Chapter 10
God in Our Beliefs

How do we understand our belief systems? Where do they lie in our bodies? Probably one of the greatest challenges we face is understanding why we believe as we do. All we know is that our beliefs reside somewhere within us. For a moment, let's examine who we really are. We know we have a physical body that responds to our five senses of seeing, hearing, feeling, tasting, and smelling. But we know that we're more than that. We really have four bodies or identities. We know the physical body exists because we can see it in the mirror, but we cannot see our other three bodies—our emotions, our beliefs, and our Soul or Spirit.

When our emotions experience trauma, we have what the medical community now calls PTSD, and a whole regime of drugs and counseling are used to clear our emotions of that experience. We also know that our connection to God is through our Spirit/Soul. This brings us to our beliefs. Sociology and psychology tell us that our belief system is based on our family teachings (intentional and unintentional), our educators in schools, our friends, and, most importantly, our culture. We grow up with the belief that we're alone in this world and that our view of the world is the only truth. Since we're alone, we assume that everyone else in other cultures must be wrong.

When I was growing up, I was taught that the Roman Catholic religion didn't practice Christianity properly; therefore, I was right and they had to be wrong. The same was true for other non-Christian religions, such as Buddhism, Islam, Hinduism, or Native American religious practices. I believed I had the truth and they had untruths. My perspective changed when I moved out of my community, went to university, and met people from a variety of different cultures, races, religions, and sexual orientations. I learned that all the people I met were just like me with the same needs and aspirations. I started out with one perspective about life, but in time my belief system expanded far beyond my initial upbringing. In the last thirty-five years since I connected my Spirit/Soul with God, my belief system has drastically expanded beyond all belief. The miracles and experiences the Lord has led me through showed me new truths that I would not have today without those real-life situations. As Job said: "My ears have heard you but now my eyes have seen you" (Job 42:5).

One of the hardest things to do is believe something different without seeing it for ourselves. This raises the question of how we as Christians can believe the teachings of Jesus when we haven't witnessed the results of His teachings ourselves. Right after Jesus' resurrection, a stranger joined a couple of Jesus' followers who were walking to Emmaus from Jerusalem. The discussion centered on the death and resurrection of Jesus. The two men were trying to wrap their heads around the possibility of anyone coming back from the dead. Their belief systems just couldn't accept such a thing as true. Even Jesus' presence with them wasn't enough, and their eyes were blind to His presence walking with them. Then Jesus rebuked their unbelief: "How foolish you are, and how slow to believe all that the prophets have spoken! Did not the Messiah have to suffer these things and then enter his glory?" (Luke 24:25–26). Finally, they recognized Jesus when He broke bread with them. At that point, they not only heard Jesus, but they saw Him and believed.

Belief systems are hard to change, even when we see things that challenge our beliefs. Think of one of Jesus' disciples, Thomas. Here was a man who'd been with Jesus throughout His ministry and saw Him perform the miracles of feeding the five thousand, healing ten men of leprosy, healing the sight of the blind beggar, calming a storm, and a multitude of other miracles. Thomas was with Jesus when He taught the parables, and he was there on the Mount when Jesus delivered the Beatitudes. Although he'd seen all of this, Thomas still did not believe Jesus had risen from the dead and had met the disciples in the flesh: "Unless I see the nail marks in his hands and put my finger where the nails were, and put my hand into his side, I will not believe" (John 20:25). Here was a man who'd seen and heard what Jesus said and did, but it still wasn't enough to change his belief system.

Where does that leave us? We weren't there to see the miracles and hear the teachings of Jesus, yet for centuries the Christian church has expected faith from us. We see examples in the Bible of individuals who search for God and find him in Jesus. Acts 8:26–40 describes how one of Jesus' disciples, Philip, brought the message to the Ethiopian high official who was searching Isaiah's scriptures to understand how he could connect to the Lord. Phillip was totally connected to God's Spirit, who directed him to go and intercept the Ethiopian and guide him to an understanding about Jesus' life and teachings. Jesus asks the same thing of us today. Christianity moves from person to person, one at a time. That's how the Christian church has grown over the centuries. Like the Ethiopian individual, when we search for God in our lives, someone or something comes along to show us how we can connect our Spirit/Soul with God's Spirit.

What happens when we do connect our Spirit/Soul to the Lord and we commit to following Him? We are called Christians at that point, and we claim Him as our Lord and Savior. We profess Jesus died for our sins, and we now can live a beautiful life following Christ. The Bible and tons of books written about the Christian life are available to us. We think we're on the right and true path of salvation that will lead us to heaven when we die … but are we? What has changed in our belief systems that guarantees we're leading life according to God's will for us.

I'd like to share an experience I had as a school principal in eastern Alberta that made me question how self- proclaiming Christians can veer off the path that Jesus taught. A very good female teacher on my staff was secretly having a lesbian relationship with another woman in the community. The relationship went sour and became public. Then the furor exploded. As an aside, both women also attended the same local church. One family that attended that same Christian church met me in my office to ask me to denounce this young woman's activities and get rid of her. Being a believer in Christ's teaching that we're to love our neighbor as ourselves (Matthew 22:39), I reminded this Christian family of this commandment and stated that it wasn't up to us to judge others. The last thing Christians want to hear is that they're wrong in their beliefs when confronted with Jesus' teachings to the contrary. They left my office unimpressed with what I said and started a social action group with their friends and neighbors, lobbying for a meeting with me and the teacher.

About twenty people, all members of the local Christian church, met with us in a town hall-type meeting to demand that I get rid of this teacher, because they didn't want their daughters being taught by a lesbian (even though the issue had never come up until the public break-up of the two women). I tried to support the young woman, but to no avail. The Superintendent moved her to a nearby community where she is successfully teaching to this day.

The question I've asked myself since then is this: How can Christians treat others so despicably and still say they are following Christ's teachings? I've come to believe that it's important to connect our Spirit/Soul to God, but that's just the beginning of our Christian walk. The belief system we grew up with will still be with us, and our prejudices will remain after our walk with the Lord commences. Jesus Christ's death and resurrection is the key to what's expected of us when it comes to belief systems that no longer function for us as Christians. Our job is to seek God to help us empty the beliefs that no longer support the teachings of the Lord. We need to pray that the sins, prejudices, and negativity that reside in our belief body leave and are replaced with God's light, love, and wisdom. Until we eliminate them from our belief system body, we can never really know God as we can and should.

I think we should look no further than the Apostle Peter, whose belief system was driven by his ego and the fear that he too would be crucified like Jesus if he admitted to knowing Him. Three times on the night his friend and master was betrayed he denied that he ever knew Jesus. Peter had been with Jesus from the start of His ministry, yet his belief system still couldn't accept the light and love God had for him through Jesus. In John 21:15–18, Jesus meets the disciples after His resurrection as they're returning from a fishing trip.

At supper, Jesus asks Peter three times, "Simon, son of John, do you love me?" Peter had tried to forget that he'd denied Jesus three times. We often think Jesus was just trying to determine Peter's commitment to leading His new church, but it was more than that. Peter's belief system needed some cleaning out to get rid of old beliefs so that he could receive the full light of God. He'd need this for the challenging times ahead. We too need Jesus to help us empty the trash bin of our outdated beliefs and give us new light, love, and wisdom. All three are gifts from God, who wants a pure connection with each one of us through His Spirit.

Chapter 20
God in Our Reflections

*I*n the Christian tradition, we have a period of reflection called Lent. God calls on all of us to reflect on our lives. Lent begins on Ash Wednesday and stretches through forty days of fasting, ending at the crucifixion and resurrection of Jesus. The forty days is based on the time Jesus spent in the wilderness prior to His spiritual ministry for God. Luke 4:1–10 describes the fasting and temptations Jesus endured. The first verse is the key to his experience: "Jesus, full of the Holy Spirit, left the Jordan and was led by the Spirit into the wilderness where for forty days he was tempted by the devil."

We must also be full of the Holy Spirit for a reflection on our own lives to take place. To have a full picture of our lives, we must be able to see our sins and imbalances from more than just a mortal human's perspective. We need to see through the eyes of God. Often our biases cloud our judgment of ourselves, so reflections with the aid of the Holy

Spirit are vital to living a life that both we and God can be proud of.

I'd like to share with you the life of a young man who found favor with God. His name was David, son of Jesse, and he grew up in Bethlehem. The Lord sent the prophet Samuel to anoint him king over Israel, even before King Saul died. In 1 Samuel 16:7, God said, "The Lord does not look at the things people look at. People look at the outward appearance, but the Lord looks at the heart." The story continues: "So Samuel took the horn of oil and anointed him in the presence of his brothers, and from that day on the Spirit of the Lord came powerfully upon David" (1 Samuel 16:13).

After the anointing, David was summoned to live in King Saul's palace to play a lyre, which soothed the King's anguished soul. The king had lost his special status with God, because he'd failed to do what God instructed. Here was a situation where God was no longer connected to Saul, as Saul had severed his connection with God's Spirit. Do we go our own way instead of following God's lead in our lives? How is our connection with God? Are we like King Saul, or David? Let's follow David throughout his life to see how his connection with God endured. We pick up the story in 1 Samuel 17, when the Israelites were at war with the Philistines.

The Philistines had a trump card in their arsenal. It was the giant, Goliath, and he literally scared the Israel army into a panic. David questioned: "Who is this uncircumcised Philistine that he should defy the armies of the living God?"

Well, you can imagine the ridicule that David endured from those who heard him—including his brothers. David was the last person King Saul had left in his arsenal, so he gave the green light for David to go out and do battle with Goliath. We know how the story goes. David, with just a sling shot and a stone, brought down the enemy's greatest soldier and routed the entire Philistine army. David had the power of the Holy Spirit in him, and he had the connection with God to perform a miracle that could only have happened with God and David acting together as one.

While King Saul was totally impressed with this young warrior, and even made him head of his army, he feared him and was jealous of God's anointing on David rather than himself. King Saul knew what it was like to have that spiritual connection with God, but he wanted to do it his way rather than God's way. I remember in my own life telling God that I'd follow Him and do whatever He wanted, and then rushing ahead of God. I thought I was doing it His way, but I was doing it my way and believing it was still God's way. It took me many years to develop patience and slow down to listen to that still small voice. As He says in Psalm 46:10: "Be still and know that I am God." We need to slow down from our hectic pace of life and listen to Him and follow His instructions for our lives.

Let's return to this famous man from the Old Testament. Jealousy can be a crippling imbalance in any person's life, but King Saul had it really bad. He continually plotted to kill

David, even though he knew that all the battles that had been won were due to David's ability to lead the army to victory. David could have killed Saul on different occasions, but he refused. His high regard for the king wouldn't let him take revenge or the crown, because he had that connection with God that gave him wisdom. David even lived among the Philistines to stay clear of Saul. Eventually, King Saul was killed in battle, along with David's best friend, Jonathan.

Even though King Saul had tried to kill him on numerous occasions, David grieved deeply for him, because he was God's anointed king. Initially, the people of Judah asked David to be their king, and once again he was anointed. Lots of political intrigue ensued before he was finally made king over the rest of Israel seven years later. In 2 Samuel 7:8–11, the Lord speaks through Nathan the prophet, who had a direct connection with God's Spirit:

> This is what the Lord Almighty says: I took you from the pasture, from tending the flock, and anointed you ruler over my people Israel. I have been with you wherever you have gone, and I have cut off all your enemies from before you. Now, I will make your name great, like the names of the greatest men on earth. And I will provide a place for my people Israel and will plant them so that they can have a home of their own and no longer be disturbed. Wicked people

will not oppress them anymore, as they did at the beginning and have done ever since the time I appointed leaders over my people Israel. I will also give you rest from all your enemies.

During his forty years as king, David continued to defeat the enemies around him and brought peace on many fronts. David proved to be one of the greatest people to live, especially when we consider the multitude of psalms he wrote during his lifetime. He was indeed blessed and loved by God, and God was totally dedicated in His faith in David. David understood that his success didn't come by his own actions, but by the blessing God gave him in every situation.

But all these blessings weren't enough to satisfy him as a person. He had at least two wives, but that didn't seem to stop him when his wandering eye spotted another beautiful woman (2 Samuel 11). Her name was Bathsheba, and she was already married to a soldier, Uriah, in David's army. David just had to have her too, so he committed adultery with her. David figured no one would ever know of this lustful encounter, but things didn't go in David's favor. Bathsheba got pregnant with his baby. Now David had to figure out how to get out of the predicament he'd gotten himself into.

He summoned Uriah home, hoping he'd visit his wife and make it look like it was his child. Well, Uriah didn't play it out as David wanted. He stayed with the other soldiers instead of going home. When that little ploy didn't work, David told

Uriah to return to the battle, but he secretly instructed his general to make sure to send Uriah to the front lines, with the hope he'd be killed in battle. This plan worked for David. With Uriah dead, there was nothing to stop David from summoning Bathsheba to the palace so that he could marry her.

Time has a way of catching up with the sins we commit in darkness, exposing them in the light. A baby son was born to Bathsheba, but he became ill. God sent Nathan the prophet to admonish David for the sin he'd committed:

> Why did you despise the word of the Lord by doing what is evil in his eyes? You struck down Uriah the Hittite with the sword and took his wife to be your own. You killed him with the sword of the Ammonites. Now, therefore, the sword will never depart from your house, because you despise me and took the wife of Uriah the Hittite to be your own. This is what the Lord says: "Out of your own household, I am going to bring calamity on you. Before your very eyes I will take your wives and give them to one who is close to you and he will sleep with your wives in broad daylight. You did it in secret, but I will do this thing in broad daylight before all Israel." (2 Samuel 12: 9–12)

David was convicted and confessed his sin to the Lord. Nathan responds: "The Lord has taken away your sins. You are not going to die. But because by doing this you have shown utter contempt for the Lord, the son born to you will die" (2 Samuel 12:13–14).

The story doesn't end there. Out of King David's dark night of the soul comes one of the most amazing psalms ever written by him:

> Have mercy on me, O God, according to your unfailing love; according to your great compassion blot out my transgressions. Wash away all my iniquity and cleanse me from my sin. For, I know my transgressions, and my sin is always before me. Against you, you only, have I sinned and done what is evil in your sight; so you are right in your verdict and justified when you judge. (Psalm 51)

At some point in our lives, we have to face ourselves and our sins. God expects us to confront and learn from them. David was a man anointed by God to be king, and up to this point in his life he'd lived according to God's directions, but then he fell off the wagon. Even though he was a man following God's directions, he failed because his ego climbed into the driver's seat of his life and led him down a road of catastrophe. God told David what was going to happen, but like all of us, he thought he could change God's mind. He spent days in prayer, refusing to eat or be consoled. To the amazement of all, when the baby died, David quit praying, got dressed, ate, and carried on with life as if nothing had happened. From my own experiences of the dark night of the soul, he entered a new relationship with the Lord.

When my Spirit/Soul connected with God's Spirit, a new life began. God no longer had to speak through others to give me messages. His still small voice was always there for me to hear when I turned to Him in prayer and meditation. After the disaster in David's life, he also began a new relationship with the Lord. Challenges don't just go away when you have that pure connection with God. What changes is how we deal with life's challenges. Wisdom comes to us when we connect with God. When we look at the last part of King David's life, we see how he deals with the challenge to his crown when his son rebels and forces him to either fight or walk away. He wouldn't kill his own son for the coup d'état, so instead he abandoned the crown and went into exile. He realized he'd made a mess of his life and accepted responsibility for his actions. In the end, God didn't take the crown from the anointed David, but He continued to love David without question.

The lesson we must take from this is that God will always love us no matter what we do; however, our sin and mistakes will always come back to bite us in some fashion. Our reflections at this time are God's command to us to recognize our mistakes and deal with them. Like David, we may have residual issues throughout our lives that act as reminders to put our egos in the backseat and put God in the driver's seat of our life vehicle.

The story of David wouldn't be complete without seeing how God can bring beauty out of adversity. David did have another son with Bathsheba, and his name was Solomon. He went on to follow David as King of Israel and was known to be the wisest king who ever existed. Amazing things can happen when we use our reflections on our lives to build a connection to God that can help us become the individuals He means for us to be. Let us receive the wisdom that God has for us.

Chapter 21

God with Us in Betrayal

Living with God activated in our lives should bring peace into our daily lives, but often that's not the case. I used to hear from various religious groups that once you accepted the Lord into your life, you would be guaranteed a place in heaven when you die. This simplified approach to God in your life just isn't rational when you live your life with many, many people who don't have that same connection to God. From my experience, being connected to God is the beginning of many challenges we have to face as Christians.

Betrayal is often the most challenging part of being a Christian. The most famous betrayal is Jesus' betrayal by Judas Iscariot. If Jesus could be betrayed by a loyal disciple, what makes us any different? Judas was one of the twelve men Jesus selected as His inner group who traveled with Him daily. Judas wasn't a latecomer; he was with Jesus in the early days of His ministry. What did Jesus see in Judas that made Him choose him in the first place? I find it hard to believe that Jesus picked him simply knowing he would later betray Him. None of His disciples had a spiritual connection with God, and several of them didn't connect their spirits to God until Pentecost, more than a month after Jesus' death and resurrection.

Judas served as the treasurer of the group, and he was accused in John 12:6 of taking money for his own needs from the treasury. We have no proof that Judas was a thief during Jesus' ministry, but the thought does paint his character darker to add to his betrayal of Jesus. From the account in Matthew 26:25, we know that Jesus was aware the night before He was arrested that Judas planned to betray Him. Luke 22:3 states that Judas was taken over by Satan. Since Satan is personified as the dark forces of the world entering into a person, we have to assume that Judas was not connected to God's Spirit, thus becoming susceptible to the negative influences of the world. We assume that when someone follows the dark side, or Satan, that they're just plain evil and deserve the worst punishment that can be meted out; however, unless we're connected to God through our Spirit with His, we too can let the dark energy forces come into our lives. When that happens, we think we're doing the Lord's will, but we're really following our own, or someone else's beliefs. Often we see Christians, just like Judas, following paths that are divisive and not unifying, which contradicts what Jesus constantly taught throughout His ministry. There have been many conjectures as to why Judas betrayed Jesus, but it really doesn't matter what his motivation was. He was following the dark side of his nature when he did the deed, but he only realized he'd chosen the wrong path after Jesus was crucified. He tried to right his wrong but failed, and his suicide followed. Have you ever wondered what would have happened if he hadn't committed suicide? What would have been his relationship with his former disciple friends?

Jesus wasn't the first person in the Bible to experience betrayal, and we have betrayal down to our present day. Genesis 6:11–22 describes how a man who was connected to God was asked to build an ark to save him and his family from the coming flood. When people do something out of the ordinary, they open themselves to betrayal. You can imagine the derision of Noah's neighbors when he started to build the ark. Betrayal was all around him. The lesson from this story is: if God is for you, who can stand against you?

Moses also suffered betrayal on different occasions, even though he freed the Israelites from slavery in Egypt, divided the Red Sea for them to cross on dry ground, and prayed and brought manna for them to eat for forty years in the desert. With all these miracles behind them, they still didn't trust the God they couldn't see. They made a golden calf that they could see and worshiped it, as recounted in Exodus 32. Once again, we see a man, Moses, connected to God's Spirit, being betrayed by the very people he helped free. Satan's dark forces took advantage of the people of Israel when Moses was up in the mountain receiving the Ten Commandments. Betrayal often seems to come out of nowhere, but is that really the case? Usually it comes from a buildup of negative thinking that leads people away from God's light. The people of Israel wanted a permanent home with good food, as they were tired of wandering in the desert and going nowhere. God was ready to cut the Israelites free and create a new nation with Moses as its head, but because Moses had that special connection with God, he wanted to save the people of Israel and continued to move them out of darkness into the light of God.

The Old Testament prophet Elijah was a man connected to God through his Spirit. He performed miracles, such as raising a widow's son from death (1 Kings 17:17–24), and he was God's spokesman at a challenging time in Israelite history. He even had control over the weather, bringing a drought and later bringing rain. At that time, the Satanic dark forces were misleading the people through the prophets of the god Baal. Elijah challenged the prophets of Baal to set up a sacrificial altar on Mount Carmel to their god. He challenged their god to send down fire to ignite the wood (1 Kings 18:20–38). The prophets failed to bring down fire from Baal, so Elijah, after soaking the wood, called on the Lord. Fire came down from heaven and burnt up the sacrifice.

With that kind of power, you'd think no one would oppose him. Wrong! While King Ahab of Israel respected and used Elijah to try to get closer to God, the same was not true of his wife, Queen Jezebel, who hated Elijah. She was his betrayer. She wanted him dead. 1Kings 19:1–5 describes Elijah fleeing for his life and feeling sorry for himself. He says to God: "Take my life; I am no better than my ancestors" (v. 4). Even a man as close to God as Elijah had doubts about what he was doing and whether he was on his own. God seemed to be really far away from him at that moment, but God is always with us, even when we don't hear or feel His presence.

God poses a question to Elijah: "What are you doing here, Elijah?" (1 Kings 19:9). Elijah's response is typically defensive when one is in the depths of despair: "I have been very zealous for the Lord God Almighty. The Israelites have rejected your covenant, torn down your altars, and put your prophets to death with the sword. I am the only one left, and now they are trying to kill me too" (v. 10). God seems to chastise Elijah for feeling sorry for himself, and He tells him to get up and get back to work. Sometimes as Christians we feel like we're the only ones doing our thing for the Lord, but like Elijah, we're reminded that we are not alone. In fact, God tells him there are seven thousand Israelites who have not bowed their knee to Baal and the dark side.

As I stated earlier, betrayal is often a part of walking the Christian path. Let me share my own story with you. I was a school principal for many years in Ontario, prior to my move to Alberta to work on a Ph.D. at the University of Alberta. After completing my degree, I decided to go back to being a principal, because that was what I felt I was good at, and it made sense to do something I was familiar with. I took a job as a K–12 principal in a community of 5,000 residents in rural Alberta. It had a resource-based economy with a high transiency rate of about 20 percent per year. I'd never lived in a community before where the value system permeated both the community and the school. There was little to no allegiance to each other or to the community itself. I was told by many people that when the time came, they would leave. No one stated that they would make their home permanently in that town. The community was isolated, with the next closest community approximately one hour away. The people were living and working in that community for one reason only— a paycheck. There were churches in the community, but none seemed to have much of an influence.

The school housed about 500 students. My introduction to the school was to be told that they'd had twelve principals over the previous twenty years. The school staff was actually very pleasant to work with, but because of the high turnover in leadership, many had either cloistered themselves to survive or had accrued power in their areas of expertise and ran their own show. There were fist fights in the hallways and a "them against us" mentality between the staff and the students, especially the older children.

My role started out as a disciplinarian, with a steady parade of children in trouble sent to the office. I established a positive reflection room to receive the students that teachers didn't want in their classrooms. With a new approach to discipline issues, I began changing the culture of that school community. I was principal of that school for five years. By the time I left, it was a school with a lot of love among the staff and among the students.

Throughout my time as principal of that school, I had the pure connection with God's light, which I shared in full measure. I can honestly say that I would never have survived working in that school and living in that community for those five years without God's light and love shining through me to everyone who lived and worked there. Now here's the kicker—that community was not my betrayer. My betrayer was a woman whose husband ran and owned a local business that employed several people. Before I came to the community, she was the powerbase behind the school, because principals came and went so frequently. She became the de facto school leader, and she got her power as president of the School Council. For the entire five years I was there, her jealousy of me and the power I took back caused her to try to find ways to move me on. She was my betrayer, but with God connected to me, she couldn't succeed until after I retired.

Even though I carried God's light and love while I was there, the light faded after I left. In the following two years after I left, they had three principals. I became the longest serving principal of that school. The message from this lesson is that God works through us, wherever we are, and it's up to us to connect with the Holy Spirit and bring His light into a world of darkness. As Christians, we do make a difference.

Chapter 22

If There Is a God, Is There a Satan?

reviously, we've discussed the nature of God. The picture that comes to mind for many people is of an old man with white, flowing hair sitting on a golden throne while directing His creation and passing judgement on mankind for their sins. What gets missed is the true nature of God. He obviously cannot be a man like the ancient gods of Olympus, who were very dysfunctional in their dealings with each other and with humankind. However, we seem to have used the Greek gods of Olympus as a template for our own beliefs about God.

We know God is a Spirit with the power to create the entire universe, including us. God is the master physicist. When you look at the complexity of everything He has created, how can you believe He is a dysfunctional being like the Greek gods? But that is precisely what we have done in our religions since the beginning of time. If God is pure love, how did our world get into such a disastrous state? How could a God of love create a creature as evil as Satan? His origin, according to the Bible, was as an archangel who became a fallen angel because he decided to go his own way and create a war with God. He battled first in heaven, and then was banished to earth to do his evil deeds.

This story has been told to us for eons by our religious leaders; however, the story didn't end there, but continued down through the ages as a fight between God and Satan for the souls of all the people on earth. Up until the invention of the Gutenberg Printing Press in the Middle Ages, all writings, including the Bible, were written by hand and translated from original texts that were written in Aramaic and Greek. From that time until a couple of hundred years ago, only the wealthy and privileged few, including the church leaders, could read and write. You've probably heard that knowledge is power. For centuries, the average person relied on the select few who could read to tell them what the Bible said. Today, many people still rely on others to interpret what God is saying to the people in the biblical texts. Very few even seek God's message for them through a total connection with God's Spirit to their own Spirit/Soul. Where is the still small voice of God directing their lives? Let's take a look at how this world and its people have gone so badly off the rails.

It all begins with our perception of who God is and who Satan is. There are only two references to "Satan" in the

Old Testament, but he's referred to as a serpent in Genesis when he tempts Eve in Genesis 3:1. The first time we hear Satan's name is in the story of Job, which was shared in a previous chapter. This is a story of how a person's faith in God must prevail, even during challenging times. In this story, Job and God appear to have human qualities to make them more relatable to the people hearing, and eventually reading it. However, we need to remember that God is a Spirit, and Satan is also a spirit. There's a major difference between God and Satan. God is light, and Satan represents the dark side. As well, God in His creation gave humans free choice to either follow the light or follow the darkness. The light of God represents the pure connection with God that Jesus had. We can also choose to follow our own ways, with our ego firmly in control. This is the way of darkness, or the personification of Satan.

Satan seems to have become a prominent part of the New Testament scriptures. Jesus was even accused of healing people using Satan's power. It's always amazing when God gives us a miracle. It's rarely attributed to God, but to some other source. Why do we have such a hard time recognizing that God is Alive and Well today and throughout all of history? Jesus asked a very profound question that we should also answer.

> Every kingdom divided against itself will be ruined, and every city household divided against

itself will not stand. If Satan drives out Satan, he is divided against himself. How then can this kingdom stand ... But if it is by the Spirit of God that I drive out demons, then the Kingdom of God has come upon you ... Whoever is not with me is against me, and whoever does not gather with me scatters. (Matthew 12:25–26, 28, 30)

Abraham Lincoln also quoted Jesus when he said, "A house divided against itself cannot stand." We're at a crossroads in this world today, because we're a house divided against itself. On the one hand, we have God asking us to connect with Him and live in the light He provides for us. On the other side of the house is Satan's dark side, which is governed by greed, lust, hatred, and division. For a house to stand, we must decide whether we want to live in the half dedicated to God's love or Satan's fear. How did we get so far from God that we don't even recognize Him and who He's meant to be in our lives? We have to go back to the beginning of time for our answer to that question.

We must always remember that God gave a piece of His Spirit in the form of a Spirit/Soul to each human at birth, and it will be with that person until the day of death when they return to the Creator God or, as many wish to call it, heaven. God's plan for humans was for each one to make the choice in their life to turn on the spiritual light switch and connect with Him. At the fall in Genesis 3, Adam and

Eve decided they wanted more in their lives and opened the door to their egos becoming their guiding principles. At this point, God's Light and Love was rejected, and the dark side of people's nature, or Satan's darkness, was given birth in the human race. Adam and Even saw the disastrous results of their selfish decision when one of their sons killed the other.

In Genesis 4:1–7, we learn that Abel was a shepherd, and Cain was a farmer who grew crops. For some reason, God was pleased with Abel's offering but not Cain's. At this point, the dark side took over Cain. God was challenging Cain to connect his Spirit/Soul with Him. The Lord said to Cain, "Why are you angry? Why is your face downcast? If you do what is right, will you not be accepted? But if you do not do what is right, sin is crouching at your door; it desires to have you, but you must rule over it" (vs. 6–7). This is the same question God asks each of us when we choose to do something from the dark side instead of from God's way. We know the end result of Cain's choice—he killed his brother and lost his way.

Jesus taught many parables to illustrate what life is like when we connect with God and follow His light and love. He liked to tell stories about farming, as most of His followers down to the present day can understand them. In Mark 4:3–20, He tells the story of a farmer planting seeds. The seeds land in different places: on paths, in rocky places, among thorns, and finally on good soil. After the parable, which Jesus left for everyone to figure out, His disciples asked for an interpretation. Jesus gave this description:

> The farmer sows the word. Some people are like seed along the path, where the word is sown. As soon as they hear it, Satan comes and takes away the word that was sown in them. Others, like seed sown on rocky places, hear the word and at once received it with joy. But since they have no root, they last only a short time. When trouble or persecution comes because of the word, they quickly fall away. Still others, like seed sown among thorns, hear the word; but the worries of this life, the deceitfulness of wealth and the desires for other things come in and choke the word, making it unfruitful. Others, like seed sown on good soil, hear the word, accept it, and produce a crop—some thirty, some sixty, some hundred times what was sown. (vs. 14–20)

Jesus' description shows us Satan's true nature. People have been drawn away from God's connection of light by Satan's darkness, which appears to us in worries or fear, the deceitfulness of materialism, or just the ego dragging us away and down the "rabbit holes" of our lives. The darkness of Satan appears to be much more adventuresome, and God's way appears less glamorous. The Apostle Paul put it best: "And no wonder, for Satan himself masquerades as an angel of light. It is not surprising, then, if his servants also masquerade as servants of righteousness. Their end will be what their actions deserve" (2 Corinthians 11:14–15).

When darkness pretends to be light, who is really in control of this planet and the people living on it? In the beginning days of the twenty-first century, we've seen a huge increase in the dark energies across the earth. Ever since World War II, we've seen a major rise in hatred, murder, and all manner of despicable acts of genocide, which has produced fear in the hearts of people around the world. It would appear that Satan's dark energy is winning the battle for the hearts and minds of the people, and God's light and love are losing. I would beg to differ. Observe people around the world showing compassion and love after these vile actions. People are coming together to stand as one for God's light and love.

Darkness can never win, because when you turn on a light switch as you enter a room, the darkness disappears. Have you ever been in an underground cave where the darkness is pitch black? What happens when you light a match? The whole cave is lit, and you can see everywhere. God's light is like that. In Revelation 20:2–3, we're shown God's plan for the darkness of this world: "He seized the dragon, that ancient serpent, who is the devil, or Satan, and bound him for a thousand years. He threw him into the Abyss, and locked and sealed it over him, to keep him from deceiving

the nations anymore until the thousand years were ended."
The dark side is fighting to maintain its hold over the earth
and mankind, but God is turning on His light switch through
His connections with people's Spirits/Souls to rid the Satan
darkness once and forever. This is the message of hope for all
humankind, and peace around the world is closer than it has
been for eons of time. We are the generation of God's light
and love.

Chapter 23

God and the Energy to Heal

Healing is a major theme throughout the Bible from the very beginning of time, as it is mentioned 164 times. When humans first entered this earth, they were given a pure spirit that was totally connected to God. The Lord also gave us free will to live as we choose. With all that freedom, we decided that we really didn't need God to live on this earth; however, there was a price to pay for choosing our own life paths over His. Thus began the downward decent into serious social and psychological issues, and the deterioration of our physical bodies. We can no longer live as long as 969 years like Methuselah, as reported in Genesis 5:27. Now if we live to one tenth of that age we're lucky.

If God originally made these bodies to live for hundreds of years, what is stopping us from crossing the century mark with bodies that would appear to be half that age? If accidents don't cause our deaths, disease or some type of body failure will bring about our demise. When I look at my own life, I marvel that I'm still on this earth in physical form. Previously, I described a skiing accident that should have led to my death thirty years ago, but I received a miracle healing directly from God. That's just one incident in my life that should have ended it. I can count five times when I could have lost my life. Two near-fatal accidents come to mind. The first occurred when I was around ten years of age. I was riding on the fender of our farm tractor, which my dad was driving. We were pulling a hay wagon behind the tractor. Suddenly, we hit a rut in the field, and I was thrown off the tractor and landed with my head between the front and rear tires of the wagon. When I close my eyes, I can still see the back tire rolling directly towards my head. Instinctively, I began rolling away from the tires and got out of the path of certain death.

When I began my career as a school principal, I had another near-death experience. I was driving a small sports car at the time, and another car coming at me decided to make a left hand turn right into my path. We collided head on at about fifty miles per hour. Compared to his vehicle, my small car should have meant certain death for me, but once again I was spared with just a huge cut on my forehead. Was this God intervening in my life? I really can't say for sure, but I do know He put me on this earth to tell you that He is alive and well and wants us to share His healing power. Surviving accidents has given me the opportunity to tell others about

God's love and His desire for us to return to Him with that pure connection He gave us in the Garden of Eden.

Let me share with you my personal experiences of healing when I was just eight years old. At the beginning of January, I took sick with a virulent flu that attacked my body. My tonsils became infected, and then the disease migrated to my kidneys and they began to shut down. I remember having a high fever and feeling like my legs were on fire and rising to the ceiling. My family, friends, and neighbors prayed constantly for me to get well. Matthew 18:20 was the basis of their prayers for me: "For where two or three gather together in my name, there am I with them." I was near death, and God, along with a wonderful doctor who visited me daily in my home and brought a new drug (penicillin), brought me back from death's door. During that whole ordeal, I was in bed from January to June. Often, we want to give credit to either pharmaceuticals or prayers that God answers, but it's usually not one or the other, but a combination of both. God has been very good to me and has shown various aspects of Himself/Herself over the years, and I am here today to share with you the very nature of God in a person's life.

Another profound healing experience happened that showed me the tremendous healing power of God. Approximately six months after me wife's brain tumor operation and radiation therapy, I saw my wife, who was an avid reader and writer, lose those skills entirely after the radiation. I was desperate for a miracle. I went to listen to a

Christian minister from Akron, Ohio, who came to preach and offer healing at a major Toronto service. This minister had a miracle gift of God for healing like nothing I'd ever seen before. I went up to him at the end of the service and asked for a healing prayer for my wife. Instead of offering a prayer, he reached out his hand and put it on my forehead. I really don't remember what he said, but I know I felt as if a lightning bolt had struck my head and traveled down my entire body. I went back home still tingling from what I can only describe as God's power. I touched my hand to my wife's head. For the next six months, she showed improvement. She began to learn to read again, but it was like teaching a foreign language. Did the healing last? No! Did I give up praying for a miracle healing right up to the last day of her life? No!

We don't always know or understand the bigger picture of life, and our lives sometimes have to move beyond our loved ones and friends. We don't have the mind of God when we're on this planet, and our plans and desires are not necessarily what God wants for us. When my wife succumbed to the cancer, I wept and said thank you to God for giving me the gift of my wife for twenty years. When people enter our lives, whether for a short period of time or a very long time, we must remember that each one is a gift from God. Some come into our lives to be our companions, and others are to be mirrors, reflecting back to us life lessons to be learned. But all are gifts from God.

Let's try to understand the nature of how God brings healing to us. We know that God is not just in heaven, but exists everywhere in the universe or multiverses. How do you visualize a God who is everywhere? We're told in the Bible that He is the light of the world. He is also the love and wisdom of the world. How can He be everywhere? Science is finally catching up with religion. We have fought for years to separate church and state. The state we could visualize with our five senses; however, the church asked its people to believe God through something nebulous—faith. How can one see, hear, touch, taste, or smell faith? Naturally it became easy to say that God wasn't part of the state. The growth over the past one hundred years of quantum physics caused us to question the whole concept of who we really are as humans, and the composition of everything around us. How do we understand that quantum material really is just like faith?

Quantum physics, or quantum mechanics, raises the issue of what everything is made of. We know that scientific experiments have proven that atoms, the building block of our own bodies, makes up cells, molecules, and DNA. Cellular biologists estimate that we have approximately fifty trillion cells in our bodies, and we have thousands of atoms in every cell. How wondrous God made the human body! Atoms are in constant motion and are swirling vortices. Our bodies consist of a constantly moving set of energy. Every cell in our body has a specific role to play, as outlined in our stem cells while we are still in our mother's womb. Even with this amazing body plan that God gave us, we still think we are just an individual physical body. Add to this that no two humans have the same physical features.

Quantum physics takes science to a whole new level by asserting that everything you see, including the earth itself, is made up of atoms; therefore, everything you see is just energy in a physical form. This is where science and religion come together. Scientists discovered that there is energy beyond our five senses. Over one hundred years ago, radio waves and electric waves were discovered. This was followed in the twentieth century by the discovery of X-rays and microwaves. Today, we take all of these forms of energy for granted as we talk into a small handheld device and hear a voice come back to us. Yet we seem to question the concept of waves and particles of light that exist all around us and can pass through us without us even being aware of them.

The Bible teaches us that God is light. In Genesis 1:3 God said, "Let there be light," and there was light. For today's audience, maybe God should say, "Let there be quantum light." As David says in Psalm 27:1, "The Lord is my light and my salvation—whom shall I fear?" In Matthew 5:14–16, Jesus gives a message to His disciples right after the Sermon on the Mount. It's the message God expects every Christian to follow in life:

> You are the light of the world. A town built on a
> hill cannot be hidden. Neither do people light a

lamp and put it under a bowl. Instead they put
it on its stand, and it gives light to everyone in
the house. In the same way, let your light shine
before others, that they may see your good deeds
and glorify your Father in heaven.

Let's look at the light from what we know about quantum
physics. It's invisible to the naked eye, just as Jesus tells us
to use our invisible light to help people find God. Good
deeds are the only thing people can see that show you are a
Christian, but when you accompany your good deeds with
prayer using the energy of God to accompany those good
deeds, people can then see God for themselves through that
quantum light of the Creator. How does God fit into the
picture of quantum light? Scientists have discovered that
quantum particles of light do some very strange things. By
passing a beam of quantum light through a tiny hole, it can
split and land in two different places. They have also found
that quantum particles and waves of light are not bound by
the speed of light (186,000 miles per second), but can reach
their destination instantaneously.

How often have you thought of someone and within a
few minutes they call you? Scientists theorize that packets of
knowledge can ride on a particle of light to a different location. As well, quantum light particles and waves can instantaneously speed across the universe. So what has this got
to do with God? We know from Genesis 1 that the Creator

God used His knowledge to create the earth and all things in it, including humans, using the quantum energy of light. If God is the great Creator of everything with light, then He's just as much alive and well in today's world as He was at the beginning of this earth. If we accept the twenty-first century view that God uses quantum light to carry His creation and answers to prayers, faith is no longer as hard to hold on to as it once was. I believe it helps us to accept that God is in the energy of the universe, and since we are composed of energy, we should look at healing not just from a physical perspective, but from an energy perspective.

Chapter 24
God through Sin

*A*ccording to the *Funk and Wagnalls Dictionary*, sin is a "transgression, especially when deliberate of a law having divine authority." The Bible first mentions the word "sin" in Genesis 4:7, when God addresses Cain prior to the murder of his brother Abel: "If you do what is right, will you not be accepted? But if you do not do what is right, sin is crouching at your door; it desires to have you, but you must rule over it." God's message is timeless for all humankind throughout history, and it's relevant today for our own lives. The Lord gives every person free choice to follow either His Light and Love, or our ego-driven life that leads to darkness.

If sin is transgression against a divine law, we need to consider what is meant by divine law? Until Moses received the Ten Commandments in Exodus 20:1–17, individuals such as Noah, Abraham, Isaac, Jacob, and Joseph received direct communication from God or His angels for guidance in their lives. Moses was the first to receive the divine laws. God realized that if He was going to influence His chosen people to follow the Light, He had to formalize divine laws to guide the people of Israel in their relationships with their families and the rest of the people with whom they associated.

We sometimes confuse God's divine laws with the rules that Moses set up to guide how people were to eat, dress, cleanse themselves, and conduct themselves to be servants of God and maintain their position as God's chosen ones. We must remember that every culture sets up norms and mores to live by, and transgression of them may lead to punishment and even death. Throughout history, we've taken a set of cultural norms that were meant exclusively for the people of Israel and believed they were divine laws of God. Often religious groups select some of the rules described in Exodus, Leviticus, and Numbers as divine laws that must be followed, while other rules aren't held to the same divine standard. Most of these rules were designed to preserve a special status with God. What gets lost is who God is. God is light, love, and wisdom. He's not a god of vengeance who waits for humans to make a mistake so that He can whack them. Once again, it's not God who whacks people. It's humans whacking other humans.

Let's take a few minutes to understand how God instructs people to deal with sin. In 2 Chronicles 7:14, the Lord makes this statement to King Solomon: "If my people, who are called by my name, will humble themselves and pray and seek my face and turn from their wicked ways, then I will hear from heaven, and I will forgive their sin and will heal their land." From the beginning of time, God asks His people, which includes all the people of the world, to turn from their choice of the dark side and choose the Light. Micah 7:18–19 poses the vital question we all must ask:

> Who is a God like you, who pardons sin and forgiveness the transgression of the remnant of his inheritance? You do not stay angry forever but delight to show mercy. You will again have compassion on us; you will tread our sins under-foot and hurl all our iniquities into the depths of the sea.

The Old Testament shows God intervening directly through the prophets to convince the people of Israel to turn from their ego driven dark side and accept the Lord and His light. It didn't seem to work, so we see God taking a new approach in the New Testament with the introduction of Jesus. God's plan was to show Himself through a special man who could teach the wisdom of God's way of living. As well, He worked through Jesus to show miracles of healing, raising individuals from death, and controlling the weather. John the Baptist introduced Jesus to the people in John 1:29: "The next day John saw Jesus coming toward him and said, 'Look, the Lamb of God, who takes away the sin of the world!'"

What made Jesus stand out from the average person? We know He was a human, but He had a pure spirit that was totally connected to God. The letter to the Hebrews states, "For we do not have a high priest who is unable to empathize with our weaknesses, but we have one who has been tempted in every way, just as we are—yet he did not sin" (4:15). Jesus became a high priest for us so that our sins could be forgiven. He became the intermediary between us and God.

> This is the message we have heard from him and declare to you: God is Light; in him there is no darkness at all. If we claim to have fellowship with him and yet walk in the darkness, we lie and do not tell the truth. But if we walk in the light, as he is in the light, we have fellowship with one another, and the blood of Jesus, his son, purifies us from all sin. If we claim to be without sin, we deceive ourselves and the truth is not in us. If we confess our sins, he is faithful and just and will forgive us our sins and purify us from all unrighteousness. If we claim we have not sinned, we make him out to be a liar, and his word is not in us. (1 John 1:5–10)

God established Jesus as His priest to be the intermediary between Himself and the people of the world. As the Christian church was established in the first century A.D., the leaders took the need for an intermediary seriously. Jesus was the first intermediary, and when we pray we often end our prayers with, "In Jesus' name we pray." This recognizes the need for an intermediary between us and God. The early church put a second intermediary between the people and God with the introduction of a priest, or pastor, whose role was to not only convey God's biblical messages to the people, but also listen to the confessions of sin. By the Middle Ages, confession of sins became big business for the church. They asked for penitence and money for sins to be forgiven by the priest and God. This eventually split the church and led to the Protestant Reformation, championed by Martin Luther, who was opposed to money being paid to eliminate sins. Divisions have plagued the Christian church throughout history, and now we have many denominations proclaiming Jesus as Savior and worshiping God.

What does all of this have to do with living in the twenty-first century? Sin hasn't really changed since the beginning of time; it's a transgression of divine law as outlined in the Ten Commandments and reinforced by Jesus when He was asked to name the most important commandment. He stated that we must love the Lord our God with our whole body, which includes our physical, emotional, mental, and spirit bodies, and we must love our neighbor just as much as we love ourselves. Unfortunately, when God is not connected to our lives, we cannot and do not love God or ourselves. Ignoring God and loathing ourselves is a recipe for disaster.

That's why God works so hard to bring us back to His light, love, and wisdom.

Let's look at Jesus' role as an intermediary to help us clear out of our four bodies the sins that have built up over the years. Previously, we have discussed our very nature as being made up of trillions of atoms that are really swirling energy. We have solid physical bodies, but in reality we are solid energy, or as some refer to it, frozen light. If everything is made up of either energy we can see, like ourselves, our homes, the dirt under our feet and our planet earth, or unseen energy we can't see with the naked eye, then what is reality? We know God is in every particle of quantum light, and His energy created the world, the planets, the sun, the stars, and all the multiverses. He comes to us as pure love, wanting us to experience that same pure love He has for everyone who connects with His Spirit.

Let's take a moment to examine how God deals with sin, or imbalanced energy. I'll share with you how I visualize sin, or imbalanced energy, in a person's bodies. Previously, I referred to it as dark energy in the form of black cotton balls, or black clouds, within the person. Sin can reside in all four bodies. This imbalanced energy builds up in a person from both wilfully and unknowingly doing or believing things that are opposed to the laws of God. For example, you may have grown up in a particular culture and family that doesn't follow the Ten Commandments, or perhaps you've experienced traumas that have left dark energy in your emotions.

Often the built-up sins or imbalanced energy can have a devastating effect on a person's physical body, causing a weakening of the immune system, often with deadly consequences. You can see how vitally important it is to clear the garbage of negative energy out of those four bodies.

The Bible teaches that only God can forgive a person, or nation, of sins. Let's see how that actually happens when we pray for the dark energy to be released from our four bodies. This can either be done personally as you connect your Spirit/Soul with the Spirit of God, or with the assistance of an intermediary, such as Jesus or a spiritually connected person. To visualize what takes place, imagine the dark energy, black cotton balls, or black cloud, being lifted from the person's four bodies. With a prayer of thanks, it's sent heavenward to God. Since He's the God of light, when He receives that dark energy, He just turns His light on it and it just disappears. In reality, God can reconstitute it as positive balanced energy.

Why did we say "thank you" when we released the dark energy, or sin, from our bodies? Every experience and every belief we have in life teaches us something good and bad, and we should always thank God for every lesson and piece of knowledge we learn. However, those emotions and beliefs are no longer needed in our future, so rather than hanging on to them, we should send them back to God. In biblical terms, God forgives our sins! There's one final step, and that's the filling of God's light into the areas left vacant by the imbalanced energy. Connecting your spirit to the Spirit of

God and asking daily to be filled with light, love, and wisdom is vital to prevent the sin and imbalanced energy from ever entering you again. It's a new life that can only be described as giving purpose to being on this earth.

Chapter 25
God in the Earth

Genesis 1:1 describes the beginning of time as we know it: "In the beginning God created the heavens and the earth." From our previous discussion, we know that God created everything from Light Energy: "And God said, 'Let there be light,' and there was light. God saw that the light was good, and He separated the light from the darkness" (Genesis 1:3–4). These scripture verses show how God used quantum light to create not only the earth, but the planets, stars, and everything in between. Einstein's theory that everything is composed of energy helps us understand how God created all things, but He continues that creative process to this day.

We live on a thin crust that sprouts all kinds of life, but beneath our very feet lies a sea of molten magma that shows itself every now and then as liquid rock spewing out of a volcano. God continues to build the earth through volcanoes, building the future mountains of the earth. Even our continents float on that same sea of magma. Every now and

221

again they bump up against each other, and earthquakes result. We see mountains rise to new heights as the rock is pushed up from below.

The earth is also a gigantic magnet, with a North and South Pole that also respond to internal stresses as God's creation continues to evolve. Movement of the North and South Pole, which has happened over the past twenty years, creates new stresses for the surface dwellers of earth. Recently, along with human pollution, the earth's weather patterns are changing, and all earth's life must adapt to the creation changes or die off. Archeology and paleontology show periods of time in earth's history when life was completely wiped out, such as the extinction of the dinosaurs. In Genesis 6, we read about how God saved Noah and his family when the rest of the human race was wiped out by rain and floods.

God instructed Noah to build an ark to save his family and all the species of life on earth. After the flood, God made a promise through a rainbow that He would never destroy humankind again, and He hasn't. Sadly, mankind hasn't been as generous to his fellow human beings. Consistently, for thousands of years, he's tried to do just that through wars and even genocide. If God won't destroy all humans, why would men and women, made in His image, try to destroy each other? That's a question religion has asked for thousands of years. Many practices have been put into place to deal with all that evil, and forgiveness has become big business. The churches have lost their power to offer forgiveness to their followers, so today our forgiveness comes in the form of a pill from pharmaceutical companies. Whether it's to ameliorate our declining physical health, the corruption of our emotional or spiritual bodies, or our skewed belief systems, humans have been running away from God rather than to Him for healing.

What's missing is our relationship with the rest of God's creation: the earth. The planet on which we live and gain our sustenance is just as important to us as even our own life. Without a positive relationship with earth, we wouldn't be alive. We owe everything to Mother Earth. Quantum physics informs us that earth is composed of atoms, just like us. Even though it appears solid like us, it's composed of swirling energy. Isaiah describes God the Creator in divine terms: "Holy, holy, holy is the Lord Almighty; the whole earth is full of His glory" (Isaiah 6:3). This verse describes God as being in every atom and molecule of the entire planet. If this is true, how do we fathom the size of God? Even King Solomon, who built a temple to God, questioned this: "But will God really dwell on earth? The heavens, even the highest heaven, cannot contain you. How much less this temple I have built?" (1 Kings 8:27).

Throughout history, religions have tried to construct buildings in which they call on God to reside. What seems to be missed is the need for God to be the God of all the earth, and not just in the beautiful temples, churches, and cathedrals of the world. God resides in humans, plants, trees, animals, birds, reptiles, and even the insects that crawl upon the earth. For centuries, the indigenous people understood the relationship that exits between Mother Earth and everything else around them. They knew that to survive they had to work in communion with all things. Everything was a gift from God and was to be honored. The ego and selfish nature had no place in life. All things and all people were considered equal. While this may appear as a utopian view, the indigenous had a balanced view of their place in God's creation, so they honored the earth. This system of balance with God's creation broke down when the conquering European peoples rejected the indigenous approach and replaced it with their ego driven side.

Throughout history, God's light and His place in this world has been pushed aside by the selfish interests of invaders, which corrupted the balance that existed before their arrival. Most invaders sought to steal the land of the residents, or take for themselves the riches of the people and the resources of the land. This continues to the present day. War is still perpetrated on people who have little power, so they become victims. When we look at the various parts of the earth, we see areas where many wars have been fought, while other areas remain pristine and battle-free. Have you ever wondered how the earth feels about all the wars and blood spilled on her ground in the name of greed and ego? If the planet earth is composed of the same energy as us, what effect are we really having on this beautiful blue and green gem in the heavens? Isaiah 24:19–20 best describes the agony of our earth:

> The earth is broken up, the earth is split asunder, the earth is violently shaken. The earth reels like a drunkard, it sways like a hut in the wind; so heavy upon it is the guilt of its rebellion that it falls—never to rise again.

How much longer can we exploit something that is a part of us? I believe the answer rests in changing our attitudes toward other humans. When we finally accept that God is in all of us through the Spirit He has given to each of us, we'll begin to offer healing to Mother Earth, who cries out to us, her wayward children. For the past two thousand years, Christians have talked about a time of real change in His creation. It appears to be a utopian view, but during this time on earth, God is asking us to change how we approach life (as I have described in this book). The Lord's Prayer asks that God's will be done on earth as it is in heaven (Matthew 6:10). That request is directed at each of us to connect our spirits with the Spirit of God. Think of how profound earth would be if everyone honored everyone else as equals. Then we could see the new earth that's described in 2 Peter 3:13: "But in keeping with His promise we are looking forward to a new heaven and a new earth, where righteousness dwells." This vision of a changed earth is also mentioned in Revelation

21:1: "Then I saw 'a new heaven and a new earth,' for the first heaven and the first earth had passed away." This is God's vision for all of us, if we rejoin His light, love, and wisdom.

Until that time, we have work to do to support Mother Earth in her desire to support our lives. We need to return to earth's composition, and, like us, she needs our healing prayers. We know she has a physical body that is under stress at the present time. What we fail to realize is that she also has four bodies like us. She has an emotional body that responds to humans. When we have thoughts and words of hatred and all manner of negative thinking, that becomes part of her emotional body as well. When we have thoughts, feelings, and words of love, they also become part of earth's emotional body. Think of thousands and thousands of years of receiving more hateful messages than loving ones, and you begin to realize how imbalanced earth's emotional body is today.

Think about Mother Earth's mental body, which also collects the thoughts, words, and actions of belief systems that don't support God's Way, but instead follow the ways of the ego. You can imagine the imbalanced nature of earth's mental body over eons of time. It may help you to understand why some parts of the world seem to have war after war, with killing and bloodshed, that seems to go on throughout all of history.

When we think of the earth's spiritual body, often referred to as Gaia, we see that the spiritual connection between God and earth is eternal. Why do we know this? Unlike humans,

Mother Earth doesn't have the freedom to choose whether or not to connect with the Creator. Since the earth has continued to absorb all of humankind's dark energy, it's up to those who are connected to God to offer prayers to empty earth's physical, emotional, mental, and spirit bodies of all the negative energy collected over the last several thousand years. God is asking us to be stewards of the earth and everything on it. As He said in Genesis 1:26: "Let us make mankind in our image, in our likeness, so that they may rule over the fish in the sea and the birds in the sky, over the livestock and all the wild animals, and over all the creatures that move along the ground." God didn't tell us to go and kill them all and use everything for our advantage, leaving nothing for our neighbor or for the needs of future generations. He asked us to be good stewards of all the earth and everything on it, and He still expects us to return to the Garden of Eden, as was His plan from the very beginning.

Chapter 26

Epilogue: Where Do We Go from Here?

By this point in the book, you're probably wondering if the information about God and His/Her relationship with humans can really be true. I've shared what I've seen, experienced, and read to aid you in making up your own mind and heart as to the kind of relationship you wish to have with God. There are times I look back on my life and can barely believe what has happened. I believe God has guided me to write this book to help you look for the miracles and guidance He/She can give. I've shared my personal experiences of connecting to His Spirit and of what He has done for me. Obviously, you won't experience life as I have. God will unfold your life in the miracles you need to live effectively. Miracles happen every day, so why shouldn't you be the one to see them yourself?

The key to understanding God is to see Jesus. He is regarded by Christians as the greatest teacher of life to ever exist. He was a man who believed in the equality of every person, no matter who they were or their skin color, culture, or religion. Going all the way back to the early times of Israel, when they received the Ten Commandments in Exodus 20:16–17, God pointed out how we should treat our neighbor, which includes everyone on earth: "You shall not give false testimony against your neighbour. You shall not covet your neighbour's house. You shall not covet your neighbour's wife, or his male or female servant, his ox, or donkey, or anything that belongs to your neighbour." Jesus picked up God's message in Matthew 5:44–45 when he stated, "But I tell you, love your enemies and pray for those who persecute you, that you may be children of your Father in Heaven." He went further when asked what the greatest commandment from God was: "Love the Lord your God with all your heart and with all your soul and with all your mind and with all your strength. The second is this: Love your neighbour as yourself" (Mark 12:30–31). These two commandments guide me in life. I know there are people who "get under your skin" by what they say and do. It's not my job to judge them but just to send them my love. Can you honestly say that your enemies deserve your prayers of light and love instead of your condemnation? You don't have to be perfect yourself to do this. We're all flawed individuals, but God asks us to rise above our pettiness and just send them His light. Let go and let God do the miracles in that person's life.

I take approximately one and a half to two hours a week to meditate in prayer. By becoming still in a quiet room, I'm able to connect with God's Spirit and listen to what He wants me to do or say. Sometimes I can feel His immense love flow into me; it's almost impossible to describe how beautiful it is to feel Him. During that meditation time, I pray for family, friends, people around the world, and for the earth itself. I use visualization to pour God's Light, Love, and Wisdom into the people for whom I pray. When praying for people around the world, I see myself above the different countries, and I ask God to fill every person with His Light. This type of prayer answers Jesus command to not only pray for our friends, but also for our enemies. Everyone in the world deserves to experience God's Holy Spirit of Light, Love, and Wisdom in their lives.

God will continue to knock on the door to people's lives, but it's up to each individual to open that door and let God's Spirit in. Everyone has free will, but our role as Christians is to direct God's Holy Spirit to everyone in the world. With prayer and projection of God's Light, you don't have to be in close proximity to the person for whom you pray. Quantum light particle research has taught us that it can travel instantly to anywhere we send it. Every person who has connected his or her Spirit/Soul with God's Spirit has the ability to pray in power. The key for us to remember is that it's not up to us to see the results of our prayers. When we pray for another person, we must send the light out but leave it to God to work the miracle that the person needs.

What power does God work through us when it comes to nature? We know Jesus exercised power over the storm when He and the disciples were out in the boat. Luke 8:24–25 describes how Jesus just spoke to the storm and it quieted down. I have related to you how a tornado was turned back when it was about to hit my house a few years ago. I believe that pure connection with the Lord does give us power over nature.

This past year, I thought I'd see if the power of God's light would have an effect on farmers' crop yields. I was aware that the indigenous peoples of the world believe they can influence the weather through various ceremonies. I've also personally witnessed house plants respond to humans who talk lovingly to them, spreading spiritual light and seeing them grow bigger and have more blooms. I didn't discuss what I planned to do at my brother's farm this past summer, but I went out into the soybean, wheat, and corn fields to offer a prayer of Light to encourage them to grow bigger and produce more seeds for harvest. I sent a visualized message out over the fields, and in my mind's eye I saw the plants grow bigger with more seeds. I then left and waited to see if there was any increase in grain yields after the harvest. My brother still doesn't know what I did, but he reported that instead of the usual yield, he got twice as much. His one hundred bushels to the acre of wheat was the biggest crop he'd ever received. Was that because of the prayer I offered to those crops? I'll never know the full effects of God's light on the fields. If God's Light can produce bumper crops for farmers, maybe we have the future answer to the shortages that exist today in several countries.

The Bible clearly states what we as humans can do if we make that spiritual connection to God. Mark 4:30–32 describes His Power in the parable of the mustard seed:

> Again he said, "What shall we say the kingdom of God is like, or what parable shall we use to describe it? It is like a mustard seed, which is the smallest of all seeds on earth. Yet when planted, it grows and becomes the largest of all garden plants, with such big branches that the birds can perch in the shade."

Jesus was referring to us—not from a physical perspective, but from a spiritual one. In Matthew 17:20, Jesus clarifies the reality of life in the Spirit even more when he says, "Truly I tell you, if you have faith as small as a mustard seed, you can say to this mountain, 'Move from here to there,' and it will move. Nothing will be impossible for you." That statement seems impossible to believe; however, scientists are beginning to see that type of power in quantum particles of light, which can do the impossible of carrying messages instantly around the world and across the universe. For years we believed nuclear energy was the most powerful type of energy in the world. We never realized there was an even more powerful energy in quantum mechanics, and its origin is in the creative forces that built the earth, planets, stars, and even us. We are part of this creative energy, and God controls it for the few people in the world who connect their spirits with Him. The last thing God will ever allow is for those who follow Satan's dark forces to gain access to it and try to weaponize it. God's energy is the energy of love, and He will share it with His followers of light, love, and wisdom.

In summary, God is inviting men, women, and children who wish to live in His light to follow Him through the door and accept Him into their life. Only serious intent to follow Him will succeed. When you walk through that spiritual door and seek to awaken spiritually, your life will suddenly have meaning. You will discover why you came to this earth as a human and what your future purpose will be. You also must release the karma of past relationships that no longer serve a purpose for you going forward. Furthermore, you carry a lot of baggage in your emotional, mental, and spiritual bodies that must be released to God. An empty vessel can be filled with God's light, love, and wisdom when you release the sin and imbalanced energy in those three bodies.

I would suggest visualizing the imbalanced energy as black cotton balls leaving your bodies and returning to God, where He can take it and turn His light on to restore it to light. This requires sincere prayers to clear out the energy you no longer need in your life. This doesn't mean you won't collect new imbalanced energy, or sin against someone or something. Cleansing our bodies should be an ongoing procedure. Make sure to visualize God's light entering and filling your bodies after clearing out the imbalanced energy. Many of the problems you have in your physical body are the result of the imbalanced energy in your emotions, belief systems, and soul. Clearing out the imbalanced energy in the other bodies often results in better health in your physical body.

One of the additional benefits of our spiritual connection to God is our ability to connect to our physical bodies and, in particular, the cells. You'll discover that the ability to communicate with your cells, which are normally on auto pilot, provides information for health. What most people don't realize is that when someone prays for healing, it's not the person who prays that brings healing. The person who prays for another is really connecting with the other person on a spiritual level. It's a soul to soul communication instructing the person's immune system to activate healing. As was mentioned in the chapter on prayer, visualizing a person in perfect health sends the message to the receiving individual about what they must do at the cellular level to answer the prayer. Our bodies can be compared to a computer. Every now and then the programs in the computer become corrupted and problems arise. Usually, we just have to turn the computer off and then back on to return the system to full functionality. This same thing happens when we receive prayers that are energetically sent. The result is a reset of the human body system. The beauty of this is that our bodies will live much longer. We may not reach nine hundred plus years, but we can definitely extend our present lifetime.

We are God incarnate on this earth, and Jesus tried to tell us that we are much more than we think we are. Our task is to connect with God and be His creators on earth. Each of us has a purpose, and it's up to us to connect with Him and discover that purpose.

My walk with the Lord has been going on for thirty-five years, and I'm still learning from Him. Don't expect Him to download all the knowledge and skills you'll need over the next few years all at once. He will give you what you need for each day of the rest of your life. Your future is individually yours to live and explore, and no one else has control over it … not even God. You are a free spirit with free choice. God will never force His will on you. He will just stand at the door of your life and knock:

> Ask and it will be given to you; seek and you will find; knock and the door will be opened to you. For everyone who asks receives; the one who seeks finds; and the one who knocks, the door will be opened. (Matthew 7:7–8)

My blessings go out to you on your quest to put real meaning into your life and find your individual path forward. Always remember, GOD IS ALIVE AND WELL!

References

Braden, Gregg. *The Spontaneous Healing of Belief*. Carlsbad, CA: Hay House, 2008.

Brennan, Barbara. *Hands of Light: A Guide to Healing Through the Energy Field*. New York, NY: Bantam Books, 1988.

Burney, Diana. *Spiritual Clearings: Sacred Practices to Release Negative Energy and Harmonize Your Life*. Berkeley, CA: North Atlantic Books, 2009.

Eden, Donna and David Feinstein, Ph.D. *Energy Medicine: Balancing Your Body's Energies for Optimal Health, Joy, and Vitality*. New York, NY: Penguin Random House, 2008.

Dossey, Larry. *Healing Words: The Power of Prayer and the Practice of Medicine*. New York, NY: HarperCollins Publishers, 1993.

Elkins, David N., Ph.D. *Beyond Religion*. Wheaton, IL: Quest Books Theosophical Publishing House, 1998.

Emoto, Masaru. *The Healing Power of Water*. Carlsbad, CA: Hay House, 2004.

Feinstein, David, Ph.D., Donna Eden and Gary Craig. *The Promise of Energy Psychology.* New York, NY: Penguin Random House, 2005.

Ford, Debbie. *Why Good People Do Bad Things: How to Stop Being Your Own Worst Enemy.* New York, NY: HarperCollins Publishers, 2008.

Gerber, Richard, M.D. *A Practical Guide to Vibrational Medicine: Energy Healing and Spiritual Transformation.* New York, NY: HarperCollins, 2000.

Gerdes, Lee. *Limitless You: The Infinite Possibilities of a Balanced Brain.* Vancouver, BC: Namaste Publishing, 2008.

Harper, Tom. *The Uncommon Touch: An Investigation of Spiritual Healing.* Toronto, ON: McClelland & Stewart, Inc., 1994.

Laibow, Dr. Rima. *Clinical Applications: Medical Applications of Neurofeedback. Introduction to Quantitative EEG and Neurofeedback.* Burlington, MA: Academic Press, 1999.

Laszlo, Ervin. *The Self-actualizing Cosmos: The Akashic Revolution in Science and Human Consciousness.* Rochester, Vermont: Inner Traditions, 2014.

Lipton, Bruce H., Ph.D. *The Biology of Belief: Unleashing the Power of Consciousness, Matter & Miracles.* Carlsbad, CA: Hay House Inc., 2005.

Lipton, Bruce H., Ph.D. and Steve Bhaerman. *Spontaneous Evolution: Our Positive Future.* Carlsbad, CA: Hay House Inc., 2009.

Loyd, Alexander, Ph.D. and Ben Johnson, M.D. *The Healing Code*. New York, NY: Hachette Book Group, 2010

Myss, Caroline, Ph.D. *Anatomy of the Spirit: The Seven Stages of Power and Healing*. New York, NY: Harmony Books, 1996.

Nelson, Dr. Bradley. *The Emotion Code: How to Release Your Trapped Emotions for Abundant Health, Love and Happiness*. Mesquite, NV: Wellness Unmasked Publishing, 2007.

Schwartz, Gary E., Ph.D. and William L. Simon. *The Energy Healing Experiments: Science Reveals Our Natural Power to Heal*. New York, NY: Atria Books, A Division of Simon & Schuster, Inc., 2007.

Shapiro, Deb. *Your Body Speaks Your Mind*. Boulder, CO: Sounds True, Inc. 2006.

The Holy Bible, New International Version. Grand Rapids, Michigan: Zondervan, 1975. (Most Bible quotes are taken from this Bible translation unless specified as KJV)

The Holy Bible, King James Version. Grand Rapids, Michigan: Zondervan, 2000.

Tiller, William, Ph.D.,Dibble, Jr., Walter E., Ph.D., Kohane, and Michael J., Ph.D. *Conscious Acts of Creation: The Emergence of a New Physics*. Walnut Creek, CA: Pavior, 2001.

Twyman, James F. *The Moses Code: The Most Powerful Manifestation Tool in the History of the World*. Carlsbad, CA: Hay House, 2008.

Walker, Robert W., Ph.D. *How Belief Systems of Classroom Teachers Affect Mandated Change*. Edmonton, AB: Unpublished thesis, University of Alberta, 1999.

$\mathscr{Appendix}$ $\mathscr{A}$

Thirty-two years ago during Dr. Robert Walker's wife's illness with a cancerous brain tumor, God asked him to create a Christian Board Game, *Mount Zion*, to show how to respond as a Christian to real life situations. Robert responded to God's call to build a game in the same way Noah probably responded when God asked him to build an ark. "You have got to be kidding, Lord!" As incredulous as Robert found the divine request, he felt the huge spiritual urge to follow the Lord's direction in his life. The Christian Game was to be three dimensional and depict a Christian's climb up the mountain of life to claim the Crown at the top. The spaces going up the mountain were coloured to match the cards. Yellow spaces indicated Blessings, red spaces were for Trials, and white were for Gifts of the Spirit. In between the visits to the hospital God guided Robert to create 150 Blessing Cards of everyday life experiences that would show how a Christian would respond and move him/her up the mountain. The cards were scripturally referenced so the player could go back to see what the Bible said about the issue. It wasn't until six months after his wife's passing that God brought him back to create the 150 Trial Cards that would move the player back. Robert completed the game and marketed it across North America in the following year and since that time production was stopped due to insufficient funds to keep it going. Over the intervening years Robert has asked himself what was his life lesson from creating that game. First of all, creating *Mount Zion* was his therapy to heal emotionally from his wife's death. Robert also said that if even one person's life was changed because of playing the game, then it was a huge success. Also, God may not be finished with the game. Maybe the time is now to send it out into the world or maybe it won't be for another thirty years. God doesn't work on a time clock like humans but His time is always perfect.

About the Author

Dr. Walker, after thirty-six years as a K-12 school principal, returned to live in Sarnia, Ontario Canada. This was the first community that started his teaching career. It is also close to his home community, where he grew up on the family farm. Dr. Walker has always been an adventurer and a creator, who loves and values all the people he has met and worked with over his illustrious career. However, to say he was just a teacher for his entire life would be a misrepresentation of his life. Even as a principal he still found time to own and operate his own farm near Sunderland, Ontario raising cash crops. During that period of time he also completed a BA in sociology at The University of Western Ontario and a M.Ed. from the University of Toronto, also in sociology. After five principalships and twenty-four years he took a break from education to take on the role of CEO of a start-up energy company, working with investors from both Canada and the United States. Immediately following that experience he became the owner operator of a franchised food business in Halifax, Nova Scotia Canada, which he operated with his wife, Irene. Following that experience they moved to Edmonton, Alberta Canada where he embarked on a Ph.D. at the University of Alberta and completed it in 1999. His thesis, in education, studied how teachers adapt to change when they are confronted with new situations. His thesis is titled. *How Belief Systems of Classroom Teachers Affect Mandated Change.* After completing the degree Dr. Walker taught first and second year sociology at the university level. More recently he has also taught social psychology at the University of Alberta. He followed that with a return to being a school principal of three K-12 schools in Alberta for twelve years. Dr. Walker may be semi-retired at the present time but the key word is semi. Along with his writing of this book he also travels to different churches as a visiting pastor.

To write a book on God, spirituality and Christianity is not something that one can do by taking to a keyboard. Dr.

Walker was raised in a protestant church, as a child, but has been to services in almost every Christian denomination. A family crisis, in 1982 was the spiritual awakening that he describes in the book. It was as if God was waiting for him to say, "Take my life and do with it as you wish." It is difficult to describe what God did in his life to show him that He is alive and well. When we think of downloading information into a computer, the same thing happened to Dr. Walker. Information and knowledge previously unknown to him suddenly over several weeks and months became known to him. His reading of books and materials on Christianity and spirituality became almost an obsession. However, awakening spiritually does not pave the way for a rosy life. Within a year tragedy struck him. His cousin and best friend, with whom he grew up, was killed in a farm accident. That same year his father and Dr. Walker's uncle passed away. As well, that same year, a second uncle also died. That was just the beginning of his trials, as a new Christian. The following year his wife collapsed at work and was diagnosed with a cancerous brain tumor. She struggled through two operations and radiation but in the end, all his prayers didn't result in a miracle and she passed away after twenty-two months. You would think that the tragedy would be over but the following year his sister-in-law, who helped him was diagnosed with bone cancer and she passed away that same year. You would think that much tragedy in a person's life would result in anger against God and life but it had the opposite effect on him. Instead he grew stronger spiritually and God led him through one of the most amazing experiences, when he created a Christian board game called *Mount Zion*. Its purpose was to show Christians in everyday situations how they should respond to life. Dr. Walker was guided by God to create this three- dimensional board game with Blessing Cards showing the Christian response to life moving the player up the mountain and the Trial Cards moving him/ her down the mountain. The aim was to reach the pinnacle of the mountain and gain the Crown of Life. Dr. Walker often refers to this board game as the snakes and ladders of Christian living. What was amazing in this whole process was how God worked with Dr. Walker in the middle and after the passing of his beautiful wife.

Since retiring from education, Dr. Walker has spent three years researching and reading books and information on the new science, Quantum Mechanics. This book, *God is Alive and Well* is the culmination of years of life experiences and coming to an understanding that God is constantly with us in the Quantum Light, that is referred to throughout the Bible. In this book, Dr. Walker brings God and science together and as you read the book, you too will discover that God is the Great Physicist and is always with us. You will discover we are all part of God`s Light and even though it looks like everyone is alone on this planet, we are all connected to each other and also we are connected to the earth. This is a book of empowerment for every person no matter what his or her belief system is. We are all one.

CPSIA information can be obtained
at www.ICGtesting.com
Printed in the USA
LVOW12s1410200917
549410LV00001B/8/P